CHURCH REPRESENTATIO

CW00547086

Church Representation Rules 2022

This edition (March 2022)
states the Rules as at 1 March 2022

CHURCH HOUSE PUBLISHING

Church House Publishing
Church House
Great Smith Street
London SW1P 3AZ

ISBN 978 0 7151 1186 4

1985 edition published December 1984
1990 edition published January 1990
1993 edition published July 1992
1995 edition published January 1995
1996 edition published April 1996
1997 edition published December 1997
2001 edition published May 2001
2004 edition published September 2003
2006 edition published January 2006
2011 edition published January 2011
2017 edition published October 2016
2020 edition published November 2019
Reprinted with revisions August 2021
2022 edition published March 2022

The text includes amendments made
by the following enactments passed since
the 2020 edition was first published: the
Church Representation Rules (Amendment)
Resolution 2019, the Church Representation
Rules (Amendment) Resolution 2020 and the
Church Representation Rules (Amendment)
Resolution 2021.

Typeset by ForDesign

Index © Meg Davies 2019, 2021

Contents

Introduction to the 2022 Edition

New Church Representation Rules came into operation in 2020. Although they entirely replaced the previous Rules, many of the concepts remain familiar. The Rules continue to provide for church electoral rolls, annual meetings, parochial church councils, deanery synods and diocesan synods, and the House of Laity of the General Synod. But there are significant changes to the way in which the Rules are presented and to their substance.

The new Rules were completely redrafted so that they were easier to understand. They are no longer characterised by over-long sentences; provisions were broken down into more easily digestible parts. The provisions relating to parish governance are set out in a self-contained Part of the Rules (Part 9). This has made navigation around the rules easier.

One of the most significant reforms was provided for in Part 2 of the new Rules. The default position is now that the model rules for parish governance set out in Part 9 apply to each parish. But the annual meeting of any parish can make a scheme to amend, supplement or replace the model rules. This makes it possible for a parish to make governance arrangements that are best suited to the mission and life of the church in that parish. A small number of essential provisions are mandatory; and a scheme making rules for a parish has to be approved by the bishop's council who must be satisfied, among other things, that the scheme makes due provision for the representation of the laity, and that it ensures the effective governance of the parish.

Another major reform was the provision for joint councils in section C of Part 9. Under the new Rules, joint councils can now replace the individual PCCs. Where that happens the number of local bodies – and the number of meetings – is reduced and should result in a significant reduction in the administrative burdens imposed on clergy and laity.

The new Rules were designed to be compliant with recent data protection legislation; they now provide for electronic communication, for better representation of mission initiatives in the Church's structures; they enable parochial church councils to do business by correspondence; and they provide that lay people must form a majority of a parochial church council.

Since the new Rules came into operation in 2020, some amendments have been made by the General Synod. These include:

- A revised system for appeals in relation to elections held under the Rules (for example, elections to a deanery or diocesan synod). See rules 57A to 61I.

- Clarification of the term of office for co-opted members of parochial church councils. See rule M17(4).
- Removal of the automatic limit on the number of terms that a parochial representative of the laity may serve on a deanery synod, there being a limit only if the annual parochial meeting imposes one for the parish. See rule M8(5) to (7).

Basic outline of the new Rules

- **Part 1** (church electoral roll) makes provision for the compilation and revision of church electoral rolls.
- **Part 2** (parish governance) provides for the model rules in part 9 to apply to each parish. But that is subject to the other provisions of Part 2 which enable a parish to make a scheme to amend or supplement, or to replace the model rules under the procedure set out in that Part.
- **Part 3** (deanery synods) makes provision for the composition of, and elections to, deanery synods.
- **Part 4** (diocesan synods) makes provision for the composition of, and elections to, diocesan synods.
- **Part 5** (House of Laity of the General Synod) makes provision for the membership of, and elections to, the House of Laity.
- **Part 6** (appeals) makes provision for appeals against decisions relating to enrolment on a church electoral roll and elections.
- **Part 7** (disqualification etc.) makes provision for persons to be disqualified from serving as a member of synodical bodies and for the vacation of a member's seat on such a body in specified circumstances.
- **Part 8** (miscellaneous) makes miscellaneous provisions for the purposes of the Rules, including provisions relating to the handling of personal data, casual vacancies, communication by email or post and interpretation.
- **Part 9** (parish governance: model rules) contains the model rules for parish governance. These provide for matters such as annual and other parochial church meetings, elections of members of parochial church councils (PCCs) and deanery synods, the composition and business of PCCs, and the making of schemes for joint councils for "connected parishes". The model rules will apply automatically unless a parish makes a scheme under **rule 12** to amend or supplement, or to replace, the model rules.
- **Part 10** (forms) contains the forms which are required to be used for the purposes of the Rules.
- **Part 11** (index) contains an index of defined terms for the purposes of the Rules.

Summary of main features of the new Rules in operation since 2020

The new Church Representation Rules implemented a range of reforms. These included the elimination of various procedural requirements relating to parish governance, the separation into a separate part of the Rules of model rules relating to parish governance, provision enabling parishes to make their own rules (with the agreement of the bishop's council), provision enabling connected parishes to establish joint councils in place of their separate PCCs, and updating the forms. The principal reforms that came into operation in 2020 are outlined in the following paragraphs.

Revision of church electoral roll and preparation of new roll

The provisions relating to the revision of church electoral rolls and the preparation of new rolls in **Part 1** are simplified. Names no longer need to be removed from the roll during the course of the year; they only need to be added: see **rule 2**. Names are still removed, as appropriate, at the annual revision: see **rule 4**. Provision has been made to avoid a person's name incorrectly being removed from a roll: see **rule 4(8)**.

Rolls may be published electronically instead of in paper form. The roll as published must include every name entered on the roll but not other personal data (e.g. addresses). See **rule 5**.

Annual meeting

The annual parochial church meeting may now be held between 1 January and 31 May (rather than 30 April): see **rule M1**.

The annual meeting no longer appoints sidesmen; they are now appointed by the PCC: see **rule M6(6)**.

Parochial church councils – ensuring lay majority

Lay members of a PCC cannot be outnumbered by clerical members: see **rule M15(2)**. A meeting of the PCC is quorate only if the majority of members present are lay: see **rule M27(2)**.

Parochial church councils – meetings

The Rules no longer specify a minimum number of PCC meetings which must be held each year. Instead, the PCC is required to hold a sufficient number of meetings to enable the efficient transaction of its business: see **rule 23(1)**.

The Rules now expressly state who is entitled to attend a PCC meeting. A PCC may invite other persons to attend its meetings as it wishes. See **rule M24**.

Parochial church councils – conduct of business by correspondence

Provision is now made in the Rules to enable PCCs to conduct business by correspondence (whether on paper or by email) where the chair of the PCC decides that particular business can properly be conducted in that way: see **rule M29**.

Joint councils

The Rules enable the annual meetings of 'connected parishes' to make schemes establishing a joint council: see **section C of Part 9**. Parishes are 'connected' if they belong to the same benefice, if they belong to benefices held in plurality or if they are in the area of the same group ministry. A scheme establishing a joint council can transfer all the property, rights, liabilities and functions of the individual PCCs to the joint council. If a scheme does that, the individual PCCs go into abeyance and no separate PCC meetings are held: the joint council does everything. Alternatively, a scheme establishing a joint council may transfer only certain property, rights, liabilities and functions – as specified in the scheme – of the individual PCCs to the joint council. If a scheme does that, the individual PCCs continue to function alongside the joint council, with the joint council exercising only the functions that are transferred to it and the other functions remaining with the individual PCCs.

Mission initiatives

The Rules make mandatory provision for the representation of mission initiatives (i.e. initiatives that are established by bishops' mission orders) on deanery synods where the bishop so directs: see **rule 24**. They also provide for persons who worship in mission initiatives to be eligible for election to diocesan synods and the General Synod: see **rule 36** and **rule 50**.

The Rules provide for the number of habitual worshippers in mission initiatives to be taken into account – together with the numbers of parish electoral rolls – when apportioning the seats in the General Synod's House of Laity between the dioceses: see **rule 49**.

House of Laity of the General Synod

The apportionment of the number of members of the House of Laity between the provinces of Canterbury and York is no longer required to be 70:30 if the General Synod passes a resolution specifying some other proportion.

Electronic communication

The Rules make comprehensive provision for the use of communication by email: see **rule 76**. Providing an email address is optional; but if one is provided, any communication under the Rules may be sent to that email address. An email will satisfy any requirements in the Rules for a communication to be in writing. Where in the past there was an obligation to pass on addresses (e.g. by the PCC secretary to the secretary of the deanery synod), any email address given by a person must also be passed on.

Electronic voting in elections

The Rules facilitate the use of electronic voting methods in elections to diocesan synods and to the General Synod: see **rule 42(5)** and **rule 56**.

Data protection

The Rules take account of the UK General Data Protection Regulation and the Data Protection Act 2018. The Rules have been designed to avoid any need to obtain consent from individuals for processing their personal data for the purposes of the Rules. Instead, personal data can be processed in the ways required by the Rules on the basis (i) that doing so 'is necessary for compliance with a legal obligation' (as the Rules have the force of law); and (ii) so far as data includes 'special category personal data' because it reveals a person's religious beliefs, that the processing is carried out internally in the course of the Church of England's legitimate activities. Personal data contained in the published version of the electoral roll is data which 'is manifestly made public by the data subject' when he or she applies to have his or her name included on the roll and is covered on that basis.

A person who holds personal data for the purposes of the Rules must ensure that the data is held securely: see **rule 72**.

Further information and guidance about data protection for parishes is available on the Parish Resources website.

Notes to accompany the new Rules

Some editorial footnotes have been included in this edition of the Rules. These do not form part of the legal text of the Rules but are there to assist the reader in navigating and using the Rules.

PART 1

CHURCH ELECTORAL ROLL

Compilation of the roll

1 (1) In every parish there must be a church electoral roll (referred to in these Rules as 'the roll') on which the names of lay persons are entered in accordance with this Part of these Rules.

(2) A lay person is entitled to have his or her name on the roll of a parish if he or she –

    (a) is baptised,

    (b) is aged 16 or over (but see paragraph (7)),

    (c) has made one of the following three declarations, and

    (d) has duly applied for enrolment on Form 1.[*]

(3) The first declaration is a declaration that the person –

    (a) is a member of the Church of England or of a Church in communion[**] with it, and

    (b) is resident in the parish.[***]

(4) The second declaration is a declaration that the person –

    (a) is a member of the Church of England or of a Church in communion with it,

    (b) is not resident in the parish, but

    (c) has habitually attended public worship in the parish during the preceding six months.

---

[*] Form 1 may, if desired, be completed and signed electronically and submitted by email where the parochial church council has provided an email address: see Rule 76.

[**] A list of Churches in communion with the Church of England can be found in the Supplementary Material in the published version of the Canons of the Church of England (available in print from Church House Publishing or online at https://www.churchofengland.org/more/policy-and-thinking/canons-church-england).

[***] A person who resides in an extra-parochial place is to be treated as if he or she is resident in a parish which the extra-parochial place borders on: see Rule 82(2).

(5) The third declaration is a declaration that the person –

    (a) is a member in good standing of a Church which is not in communion with the Church of England but subscribes to the doctrine of the Holy Trinity,

    (b) is also a member of the Church of England, and

    (c) has habitually attended public worship in the parish during the preceding six months.

(6) A person who is entitled under this Rule to have his or her name on the roll of more than one parish is entitled to have his or her name on the roll of each of those parishes; but the following provisions specify purposes for which the person is required to choose one of those parishes –

    (a) Rule 16(2) (membership of the house of laity of a deanery synod);

    (b) Rule 33(6) (additional members of diocesan synod nominated by bishop);

    (c) Rule 36(4) (eligibility for election to diocesan synod);

    (d) Rule 50(8) (eligibility for election by diocesan electors);

    (e) Rule M8(2) (eligibility for election as parochial representative of laity);

    (f) Rule M15(6) or (7) (membership of PCC).

(7) Where a lay person, who is going to become 16 after a revision of the roll or the preparation of a new roll is complete but before the date of the annual parochial church meeting, duly applies for enrolment on Form 1, the enrolment may take effect on the person's 16th birthday.

(8) The roll of a parish must be kept and revised –

    (a) by the PCC, or

    (b) by the electoral roll officer under the direction of the PCC.

(9) Where a new parish is created by a pastoral scheme by the union of two or more former parishes, the roll of the new parish is in the first instance to consist of the rolls of the former parishes combined to form a single roll.

(10) In any other case where a new parish is created by a pastoral scheme, the roll of the new parish is in the first instance to consist of the name of every person who –

    (a) on the date when the new parish comes into existence, has his or her name on the roll of a parish the whole or part of which forms part of the new parish, and

    (b) is resident in the new parish or has habitually attended public worship there.

(11) The roll of a parish must, where practicable, specify the address of every person whose name is on it; but a failure to specify an address does not affect the validity of the entry.

(12) Where a person has provided an email address on Form 1, the roll must specify that email address.*

(13) A copy of the roll of a parish must be made available for inspection, on a reasonable request being made to the PCC; and the copy made available for inspection must include every name entered on the roll but no other personal data.

Additions to the roll

2 (1) The name of a person who is entitled to have his or her name on the roll of a parish must, subject to these Rules, be added to the roll.

(2) If additions are made to the roll, the electoral roll officer must report them at the next meeting of the PCC.

(3) A list of the names added, but no other personal data, must be made available for inspection, on a reasonable request being made to the PCC.

Revision of the roll: notice

3 (1) The roll of a parish must be revised annually, except in a year in which a new roll is prepared (as to which, see Rules 6 and 7).

(2) Notice of the proposed revision must be given on Form 2 and displayed by or under the direction of the minister –

(a) in the case of the parish church or, where there is more than one church in the parish, each of those churches, on or near the principal door, and

(b) in the case of each building in the parish licensed for public worship, in a location readily visible to members of the congregation.

(3) The notice under paragraph (2) must remain on display for at least 14 days before the proposed revision begins.

(4) In a case where the minister is absent or incapacitated by illness or for some other reason or where there is nobody who is the minister within the meaning of these Rules (see Rule 83(1)), the minister's function under this Rule is to be carried out by –

(a) the vice-chair of the PCC, or

(b) if there is not a vice-chair or the vice-chair is unable or unwilling to act, the secretary of the PCC or some other person appointed by the PCC.

---

* If a person provides an email address, any communication under the Church Representation Rules may be sent by email to that address: see Rule 76.

Revision of the roll: preparation

4   (1)   On each revision of the roll of a parish –

(a)   every addition to the roll since the previous revision (or, if there has not yet been a revision of the roll, since the formation of the roll) must be reviewed and any further additions must be made as necessary, and

(b)   a person's name must be removed from the roll in each of the following cases.

(2)   The first case is where the person has died.

(3)   The second case is where the person has become a clerk in Holy Orders.

(4)   The third case is where the person has stated in writing the wish to have his or her name removed.

(5)   The fourth case is where the person was not entitled to have his or her name entered on the roll at the time it was entered.

(6)   The fifth case is where the person –

(a)   has ceased to reside in the parish,

(b)   has not continued to habitually attend public worship in the parish during any period of six months, and

(c)   has not been prevented from doing so by illness or other sufficient cause.

(7)   The sixth case is where the person –

(a)   is not resident in the parish,

(b)   has not habitually attended public worship in the parish during the preceding six months, and

(c)   has not been prevented from doing so by illness or other sufficient cause.

(8)   The name of a person must not be removed from the roll in the fourth, fifth or sixth case unless the PCC has taken reasonable steps to establish the relevant facts.

(9)   The removal of a person's name from the roll under these Rules does not affect any right the person may have, or may acquire, to have his or her name entered again.

(10)   The revision of the roll of a parish must be completed at least 15 days, but no more than 28 days, before the annual parochial church meeting.

Publication of revised roll

5 (1) After the completion of a revision of the roll of a parish under Rule 4, the PCC must –

    (a) publish the roll in such form (whether electronic or otherwise) as it decides, and

    (b) make a copy of the roll available for inspection, on a reasonable request being made.

  (2) The period for which the revised roll is published under paragraph (1)(a) must be at least 14 days.

  (3) The roll as published, and the copy made available for inspection, must include every name entered on the roll but no other personal data.

  (4) A name may not be added to or removed from the roll between the completion of the revision of the roll and the conclusion of the annual parochial church meeting, except in so far as is necessary –

    (a) to correct an omission or other error, or

    (b) for complying with Rule 1(2)(b) and (7) (persons becoming 16).

Preparation of new roll: notice

6 (1) Notice that a new roll for a parish is to be prepared must be given on Form 3 and displayed by or under the direction of the minister –

    (a) in the case of the parish church or, where there is more than one church in the parish, each of those churches, on or near the principal door, and

    (b) in the case of a building in the parish licensed for public worship, in a location readily visible to members of the congregation.

  (2) The notice under paragraph (1) –

    (a) must be put on display at least two months before the annual parochial church meeting in every sixth year beginning with 2025, and

    (b) must remain on display for at least 14 days.

  (3) The preparation of a new roll for a parish –

    (a) must not begin before the date on which the notice is displayed under paragraph (1), and

    (b) must be completed at least 15 days, but no more than 28 days, before the annual parochial church meeting.

  (4) At every service held on each of the two Sundays in the period of 14 days beginning with the date on which the notice is displayed under paragraph

(1), the person conducting the service must inform the congregation of the preparation of the new roll.

(5) In the case of a church in which no service is held on either of the two Sundays in that period, at every service held on the first Sunday after the date on which the notice is displayed under paragraph (1), the person conducting the service must inform the congregation of the preparation of the new roll.

(6) In a case where the minister is absent or incapacitated by illness or for some other reason or where there is nobody who is the minister within the meaning of these Rules (see Rule 83(1)), the minister's function under this Rule is to be carried out by –

(a) the vice-chair of the PCC, or

(b) if there is not a vice-chair or the vice-chair is unable or unwilling to act, the secretary of the PCC or some other person appointed by the PCC.

Preparation of new roll: process

7 (1) The PCC of each parish must take reasonable steps to inform every person whose name is on the roll of the parish –

(a) that a new roll is being prepared, and

(b) that, if the person wishes to have his or her name entered on the new roll, the person must apply for enrolment.

(2) The duty under paragraph (1) does not apply in the case of a person whose name would be removed under Rule 4 if the roll were being revised; but before deciding that a person comes within the fourth, fifth or sixth case under that Rule, the PCC must take reasonable steps to establish the relevant facts.

(3) On the preparation of a new roll, the name of each person who is entitled to have his or her name entered under Rule 1 must be entered on the roll; and a fresh application on Form 1 is required from each person whose name is already on the roll.

(4) A person whose name is already on the roll is not disqualified from having his or her name on the new roll merely because he or she has not complied with the condition in Rule 1(4)(c) or (5)(c) (habitual attendance at public worship), if the person was prevented from doing so by illness or other sufficient cause.

(5) In a case where paragraph (4) applies, the application on Form 1 must briefly state why the person did not comply with the condition in question.

Publication of new roll

8 (1) After the completion of a new roll under Rule 7, the PCC must –

    (a) publish the roll in such form (whether electronic or otherwise) as it decides, and

    (b) make a copy of the roll available for inspection, on a reasonable request being made.

(2) The period for which the new roll is published under paragraph (1)(a) must be at least 14 days.

(3) The roll as published, and the copy made available for inspection, must include every name entered on the roll but no other personal data.

(4) A name may not be added to or removed from the roll in the 14 days beginning with the day on which the roll is published under paragraph (1)(a), except in so far as is necessary –

    (a) to correct an omission or other error, or

    (b) for complying with Rule 1(2)(b) and (7) (persons becoming 16).

(5) The new roll takes effect on its publication under this Rule (at which point the previous roll ceases to have effect).

Boundary changes

9 (1) On an alteration of the boundaries of parishes, the PCC of each parish from which an area is transferred must ask each person resident in that area whose name is on the roll of the parish whether the person wishes to have his or her name transferred to the roll of the other parish.

(2) Where a person answers in the affirmative –

    (a) the PCC must remove the person's name from the roll for its parish and inform the PCC of the parish in which the person now resides, and

    (b) the PCC of that parish must enter the person's name on its roll without requiring him or her to apply for enrolment.

Notification of number on roll

10 The chair, vice-chair, secretary or electoral roll officer of a PCC must, no later than 1 July in each year, give the secretary of the diocesan synod written notification of the number of names there are on the roll of the parish as at the date of the annual parochial church meeting.

PART 2

PARISH GOVERNANCE

Model Rules

11   The Rules in Part 9 apply to each parish.

Scheme for amendment

12   (1)   The annual parochial church meeting or a special parochial church meeting may make a scheme to amend or supplement, or to replace (either as a whole or in part), the Rules in Part 9 in so far as they apply to that parish.

(2)   A scheme under this Rule may not make provision which would disapply or suspend or restrict the application of –

(a)   Rule M8(4) to (8) (disqualification from nomination to be parochial representative);

(b)   Rule M13 (special parochial meeting);

(c)   Rule M14 (extraordinary parochial meeting);

(d)   Rule M15(2) and (3) (PCC: laity must outnumber clergy);

(e)   Rule M15(13) (PCC: disqualification from membership);

(f)   Rule M27(2) (PCC quorate only if majority present lay);

(g)   Rule M36 (district church council: disqualification from membership);

(h)   Rule M41 (joint council: disqualification from membership);

(i)   Rule M42(5) (joint council: laity must outnumber clergy).

Procedure for making scheme

13   (1)   A scheme under Rule 12 is valid only if it is approved by at least two-thirds of the persons present and voting at the meeting.

(2)   A scheme approved under paragraph (1) must be referred to the bishop's council and standing committee and must be accompanied by –

(a)   a copy of the resolution of the meeting at which the scheme was approved, and

(b) a statement of the number of persons attending the meeting, the number voting for approval of the scheme and the number voting against.

(3) The bishop's council and standing committee, having had a scheme referred to it under paragraph (2), may –

(a) approve the scheme without amendment,

(b) approve the scheme subject to proposed amendments, or

(c) decline to approve the scheme.

(4) The bishop's council and standing committee may approve a scheme only if it is satisfied that the scheme –

(a) makes due provision for the representation of the laity of the parish,

(b) ensures effective governance of the parish,

(c) entitles the minister to chair the annual parochial church meeting and the PCC, and

(d) makes due provision for the allocation of property, rights, liabilities and functions to the PCC in circumstances where there is a scheme for the establishment of a joint council but the parish –

(i) ceases to be connected to the other parish or parishes to which the scheme applies (see Rule M37(4)), or

(ii) is dissolved by a pastoral scheme which makes provision under section 31(1)(b) of the Mission and Pastoral Measure 2011.

(5) An amendment proposed under paragraph (3)(b) is passed only if it is approved by at least two-thirds of the persons present and voting at the annual parochial church meeting or a special parochial church meeting.

(6) A scheme under Rule 12 does not come into operation unless it has been approved by the bishop's council and standing committee.

(7) A scheme under Rule 12 comes into operation on the day specified in the scheme.

(8) Where a scheme under Rule 12 is approved under this Rule, a copy of the scheme –

(a) must be filed in the diocesan registry, and

(b) must be sent to the secretary of the bishop's council and standing committee.

PART 3

DEANERY SYNODS

Composition

14   A deanery synod consists of –

(a) a house of clergy, and

(b) a house of laity.

House of clergy

15 (1) The members of the house of clergy of a deanery synod are every clerk in Holy Orders –

(a) who is beneficed in or licensed to a parish in the deanery,

(b) who is licensed under section 2 of the Extra-Parochial Ministry Measure 1967 in respect of an institution in the deanery,

(c) who is a clerical member of the General Synod or a diocesan synod and is resident in the deanery,

(d) who is resident in the deanery and licensed by the bishop to work throughout the diocese or in more than one deanery and is not subject to a direction under Rule 17 to be a member of another deanery synod,

(e) who is not resident in the deanery but is subject to a direction under Rule 17 to be a member of the deanery synod,

(f) who holds permission to officiate, is resident in the deanery or has habitually attended public worship in the deanery during the preceding six months, and is elected or chosen as mentioned in paragraph (2),

(g) who is co-opted under Rule 18, or

(h) who is made a member by virtue of a scheme under Rule 23 or 24 (cathedrals, royal peculiars, mission initiatives).

(2) One clerk who is eligible for membership under paragraph (1)(f) is to be elected or chosen –

(a) for every ten clerks of that description, and

(b) where the number of such clerks is not divisible by ten without fraction or remainder, for the fraction or remainder.

(3) The election or choice under paragraph (2) is made by and from the clerks who are eligible for membership under paragraph (1)(f) in such manner as the bishop may approve.

(4) As soon as possible after 31 December in the year before an election of the parochial representatives of the laity to the deanery synod, the rural dean of the deanery must inform the bishop of the number of clerks in Holy Orders who are eligible for membership under paragraph (1)(f).

(5) A member of a deanery synod under paragraph (1)(f) –

(a) is elected or chosen every three years, and

(b) holds office for a term of three years beginning with the next 1 July following the date when the election or choice takes place.

House of laity

16 (1) The members of the house of laity of a deanery synod are –

(a) each parochial representative elected to the deanery synod by the annual parochial church meeting of each parish in the deanery,

(b) any lay member of the General Synod or a diocesan synod whose name is on the roll of a parish* in the deanery,

(c) each deaconess or lay worker who is licensed by the bishop to work in the whole or part of the deanery,

(d) any deaconess or lay worker who is resident in the deanery and licensed by the bishop to work throughout the diocese or in more than one deanery and is not subject to a direction under Rule 17 to be a member of another deanery synod,

(e) any deaconess or lay worker who is not resident in the deanery but is subject to a direction under Rule 17 to be a member of the deanery synod,

(f) if the bishop considers that a community in the deanery which is in the spiritual care of a chaplain licensed by the bishop should be represented in the house of laity, one lay person chosen by and from the members of the community in such manner as the bishop approves,

(g) any lay person who is co-opted under Rule 18, and

---

* A person whose name is on the roll of a guild church in the City of London is treated for this purpose as if his or her name is also on the roll of the parish in which the guild church is situated: see Rule 83(7) and (8).

(h) any lay person who is made a member by virtue of a scheme under Rule 23 or 24 (cathedrals, royal peculiars, mission initiatives).

(2) Where a person's name is on the roll of more than one parish, the person must choose one of the parishes concerned for the purposes of paragraph (1)(a) or (b).

(3) A person is eligible for membership of a deanery synod under paragraph (1)(f) only if the person is an actual communicant and is aged 16 or over.

(4) The person who is the member of a deanery synod under paragraph (1)(f) –

(a) is chosen every three years, and

(b) holds office for a term of three years beginning with the next 1 July following the date when the choice is made.

Direction to join a different deanery synod

17 (1) A clerk in Holy Orders, deaconess or lay worker who resides in the deanery and is licensed by the bishop to work throughout the diocese or in more than one deanery may be given a direction –

(a) not to be a member of the deanery synod for the deanery in which he or she resides, but

(b) instead to be a member of the deanery synod specified in the direction.

(2) A direction under this Rule may be given to a clerk in Holy Orders only by the clerical members of the bishop's council and standing committee; and, when doing so, they must have regard to the number of parochial and non-parochial clergy in the deanery in which the clerk resides.

(3) A direction under this Rule may be given to a deaconess or lay worker only by the lay members of the bishop's council and standing committee; and, when doing so, they must have regard to the number of deaconesses in the deanery in which the deaconess resides or (as the case may be) the number of lay workers in the deanery in which the lay worker resides.

(4) A person may not, as a result of a direction under this Rule, be a member of more than one deanery synod in the same diocese.

(5) A direction under this Rule may provide for –

(a) a specified category of clerks, deaconesses or lay workers (as the case may be) to choose some of their number to be members, and

(b) the term of office of a person so chosen.

Co-option

18 (1) The house of clergy of a deanery synod may co-opt as additional members other clerks in Holy Orders.

(2) The house of laity of a deanery synod may co-opt as additional members other lay persons who are actual communicants aged 16 or over.

(3) The number of persons co-opted to a house under this Rule must not exceed either 5% of the total number of members of that house or three, whichever is greater.

(4) The term of office of a person co-opted under this Rule is (subject to termination or resignation) for the lifetime of the deanery synod; but that does not prevent the person from being co-opted on one or more subsequent occasions.

Election of parochial representatives

19 (1) The parochial representatives of the laity on a deanery synod –

    (a) are elected every three years beginning with 2020 by the annual parochial church meeting of each parish in the deanery, and

    (b) hold office for a term of three years beginning with the next 1 July following the date of their election.

(2) The number of representatives to be elected from each parish is determined by a resolution of the diocesan synod no later than 31 December in the year preceding the elections.

(3) A diocesan synod may calculate the number of representatives from a parish for the purposes of paragraph (2) –

    (a) by reference to the number of names on the roll of the parish specified in the notification under Rule 10,

    (b) by reference to the number of parish churches or districts in the parish, or

    (c) by a combination of both those methods.

(4) The secretary of a diocesan synod must, no later than 31 December in the year preceding the elections –

    (a) certify to the secretary of each PCC the number of parochial representatives to be elected at the annual parochial church meeting of the parish, and

    (b) give the secretary of each deanery synod a copy of each certificate given under sub-paragraph (a) and information relating to each parish in the deanery.

List of members to be given to diocesan electoral registration officer

20 (1) The secretary of each deanery synod must, after the election of the parochial representatives of the laity to the synod but no later than the next following 1 July, give the diocesan electoral registration officer (see Rule 27) –

(a) a list of the names and addresses of the members of the house of clergy of that synod, specifying for each member the category of membership under Rule 15(1), and

(b) a list of the names and addresses of the members of the house of laity of that synod, specifying for each member the category of membership under Rule 16(1).

(2) If a person is co-opted to either house of a deanery synod under Rule 18, the secretary of the synod must give the diocesan electoral registration officer the name and address of the person.

(3) The secretary of each deanery synod must give the diocesan electoral registration officer details of any subsequent changes to the membership of the house of clergy or the house of laity of that synod.

Number of members

21 (1) A diocesan synod must exercise its powers under this Part of these Rules so as to secure that the total number of members of each deanery synod in the diocese is –

(a) no more than 150 (subject to paragraph (2)), and

(b) so far as practicable, no less than 50.

(2) The figure of 150 given in paragraph (1)(a) may be exceeded in order –

(a) to secure that the house of laity has at least as many members as the house of clergy has, or

(b) to enable the operation of a scheme under Rule 23 or 24 which was made since the most recent resolution passed under Rule 19(2).

(3) For the avoidance of doubt, the figure of 150 given in paragraph (1)(a) includes the maximum number of persons who may be co-opted as members of either house.

Scheme for variation of membership

22 (1) A diocesan synod may make a scheme to vary the preceding provisions of this Part of these Rules that relate to the membership of deanery synods so as both –

(a) to meet the special circumstances of the diocese or the deaneries, and

(b) to secure better representation of clergy or laity or both on the deanery synods.

(2) Where a scheme under this Rule has effect, the preceding provisions of this Part of these Rules, in so far as they apply to each deanery synod concerned, have effect subject to the scheme.

Scheme for representation for cathedrals and royal peculiars

23 (1) In the case of the cathedral church of each diocese (other than the cathedral church of Christ in Oxford, as to which see paragraph (2)) or, where a diocese has more than one cathedral church, each of them, the diocesan synod must make a scheme to provide for the representation on a deanery synod of –

    (a) the dean, the residentiary canons and other ministers (or any of them), and

    (b) unless the cathedral church is a parish church, every lay person whose name is on the community roll.

    (2) In the case of Westminster Abbey, St George's Chapel, Windsor and the cathedral church of Christ in Oxford, the diocesan synod in each case must make a scheme to provide for the representation on a deanery synod of –

    (a) the dean, the residentiary canons and other ministers (or any of them), and

    (b) every lay person whom the dean has declared to be a habitual worshipper and whose name is not on the roll of a parish.

    (3) A scheme under this Rule must include provision for determining the deanery synod or synods to which it applies.

Scheme for representation for mission initiatives

24 (1) Where a bishop's mission order is in force, a diocesan synod must, at the direction of the bishop or bishops who made the order, make a scheme to provide for the representation on a deanery synod of such of the persons to whom the order relates as are specified in or under the scheme.

    (2) The Code of Practice under section 84 of the Mission and Pastoral Measure 2011 (mission initiatives) must include guidance as to the exercise of functions under this Rule.

    (3) The bishop or bishops, in giving a direction under paragraph (1), and the diocesan synod, in making a scheme under this Rule, must have regard to –

    (a) the need to make due provision for the representation of the worshipping community involved in the mission initiative,

    (b) the governance of the initiative (which may, for example, take the form of a charitable body of some kind), and

    (c) the guidance referred to in paragraph (2).

    (4) A scheme under this Rule must include provision for determining the deanery synod or synods to which it applies.

Schemes: approval

25 (1) A copy of a proposed scheme under Rule 22, 23 or 24 must be given to each member of the diocesan synod at least 14 days before the meeting at which it is to be considered for approval.

   (2) A proposed scheme under Rule 22 is approved by the diocesan synod only if –

    (a) the house of bishops approves it,

    (b) in the house of clergy, it is approved by at least two-thirds of the members present and voting, and

    (c) in the house of laity, it is approved by at least two-thirds of the members present and voting.

   (3) A proposed scheme under Rule 22 which is approved by the diocesan synod must be laid before the General Synod.

   (4) If a member of the General Synod gives notice in accordance with its Standing Orders that the member wishes a proposed scheme under Rule 22 to be debated, the scheme does not come into operation unless it is approved by the General Synod.

   (5) If a proposed scheme under Rule 22 is approved by the General Synod or no notice such as is mentioned in paragraph (4) is given, the scheme comes into operation –

    (a) on the day after the end of the group of sessions during which it was laid before, or approved by, the Synod, or

    (b) on such later date as the scheme may specify.

Procedure

26 (1) A diocesan synod must make rules for the deanery synods in the diocese.

   (2) The rules must include provision –

    (a) for the rural dean and a member of the house of laity of the deanery synod elected by that house to be the joint chairs;

    (b) for the joint chairs to decide between themselves who is to chair each meeting or particular items of business on the agenda;

    (c) for there to be a secretary;

    (d) for a specified minimum number of meetings to be held in each year;

    (e) for decisions to be taken by a majority of members present and voting, except where the rules require there to be a vote by houses;

    (f) for there to be a standing committee, the membership and functions of which are provided for by the rules;

(g) for a report of the deanery synod's proceedings to be given to every PCC in the deanery.

(3) The rules may include provision for such other matters consistent with the provision required by paragraph (2) as the diocesan synod decides.

(4) The provision which may be made under paragraph (3) includes provision to impose a maximum period for which a person may serve as an officer, or as a member of the standing committee, of a deanery synod in the diocese.

(5) The provision which may be so made also includes provision to enable the lay chair of each deanery synod in the diocese to continue to hold office as such until the election of his or her successor as chair.

(6) Subject to the rules, a deanery synod may determine its own procedure.

(7) 'Lay chair', in relation to a deanery synod, means the member of the house of laity of the deanery synod who, by virtue of paragraph (2)(a), is one of the two joint chairs of the synod.

Diocesan electoral registration officer

27 (1) In each diocese, a diocesan electoral registration officer is appointed by the bishop's council and standing committee of the diocesan synod.

(2) The diocesan electoral registration officer must, subject to paragraph (4), record in a register the name and address of every member of the house of clergy of each deanery synod in the diocese (the 'register of clerical electors').

(3) The diocesan electoral registration officer must, subject to paragraph (4), record in a register (separate from the register of clerical electors) the name and address of every member of the house of laity of each deanery synod in the diocese (the 'register of lay electors').

(4) Persons co-opted as members of the house of clergy or the house of laity of a deanery synod are not to be recorded in the register concerned.

(5) Where a member of the house of clergy or the house of laity of a deanery synod has provided the diocesan electoral registration officer with an email address, the address recorded for that member in the register must include that email address.

Mission initiative roll

27A (1) Where a direction is given under Rule 24(1), the leader of the mission initiative must establish and maintain a roll (a 'mission initiative roll') on which the names of lay persons are entered in accordance with this Rule.

(2) A person is eligible to have his or her name on a mission initiative roll if he or she –

    (a) is baptised,

    (b) is aged 16 or over, and

    (c) has made a written application to have his or her name on the roll.

(3) An application under paragraph (2)(c) must include a declaration that the applicant –

    (a) either is a member of the Church of England or a Church in communion with it or is a member in good standing of a Church which is not in communion with the Church of England but which subscribes to the doctrine of the Holy Trinity, and

    (b) has habitually attended public worship as part of the worshipping community involved in the initiative during the preceding six months.

(4) A person who is eligible to have the person's name on more than one mission initiative roll is entitled to have the person's name on each of the mission initiative rolls concerned.

(5) In the case of a mission initiative which is in more than one diocese, the function of giving a direction under paragraph (1) is exercisable by the diocesan bishops concerned acting jointly.

(6) Where a direction was given under rule 29A of the Old Rules, the duty under paragraph (1) of this rule to maintain a mission initiative roll applies to the roll established under that rule; and a reference in Rules 27B to 27D to a mission initiative roll includes a reference to any mission initiative roll so established.

(7) In paragraph (6), 'the Old Rules' means these Rules as set out in this Schedule in the form it took immediately before the commencement of Schedule 1 to the Church Representation and Ministers Measure 2019.

Additions to and revision of mission initiative roll

27B (1) The name of a person who is eligible to have his or her name on a mission initiative roll must be added to the roll.

(2) A mission initiative roll must be revised by the leader of the mission initiative no later than 30 May in each year.

(3) On each revision of a mission initiative roll –

    (a) every addition to the roll since the previous revision (or, if there has not yet been a revision of the roll, since the establishment of the roll) must be reviewed and any further additions must be made as necessary, and

    (b) a person's name must be removed from the roll in each of the following cases.

(4) The first case is where the person has died.

(5) The second case is where the person has become a clerk in Holy Orders.

(6) The third case is where the person has stated in writing the wish to have his or her name removed.

(7) The fourth case is where the person was not entitled to have his or her name entered on the roll at the time it was entered.

(8) The fifth case is where the person –

(a) has not habitually attended public worship as part of the worshipping community involved in the initiative during the preceding six months, and

(b) has not been prevented from doing so by illness or other sufficient cause.

Preparation of new mission initiative roll

27C (1) The leader of a mission initiative must, no later than 30 May in every sixth year beginning with 2025, prepare a new mission initiative roll.

(2) On the preparation of a new mission initiative roll, the name of each person who is eligible to have his or her name entered under Rule 27A must be entered on the roll; and a fresh application, which must include the declaration under Rule 27A(3), is required from each person who is already on the roll.

(3) A person whose name is already on a mission initiative roll is not disqualified from having his or her name on the new roll merely because he or she has not complied with the condition in Rule 27A(3)(b), if the person was prevented from doing so by illness or other sufficient cause.

(4) In a case where paragraph (3) applies, the application must briefly state why the person did not comply with that condition.

Notification of number on mission initiative roll

27D The leader of a mission initiative must, no later than 1 July in each year, give the secretary of the diocesan synod written notification of the number of names there are on the mission initiative roll as at 30 May in that year.

Casual vacancies

28 (1) A casual vacancy* among the parochial representatives elected to a deanery synod must be filled as soon as practicable after the vacancy occurs.

---

* 'Casual vacancy' includes the case where there is a vacancy because not enough candidates were nominated to fill the places available: see rule 83(9).

(2) Where the annual parochial church meeting is not due to be held within the two months following the occurrence of the vacancy, the vacancy must be filled by the election by the PCC of a person who is qualified to be elected as a parochial representative.

(3) An election to fill a casual vacancy among the parochial representatives elected to a deanery synod is, where possible, to be held at a time which will enable all casual vacancies among the parochial representatives so elected to have been filled by the time of the next election to the House of Laity of the General Synod; but no such election is invalid merely because such a casual vacancy is not filled.

(4) The secretary of a PCC must give a return of a parochial representative of the laity elected to fill a casual vacancy on the deanery synod –

(a) to the diocesan electoral registration officer, and

(b) to the secretary of the deanery synod.

PART 4

DIOCESAN SYNODS

MEMBERSHIP

Composition

29 (1) A diocesan synod consists of –

    (a) a house of bishops,

    (b) a house of clergy, and

    (c) a house of laity.

(2) The bishop of the diocese is the president of the diocesan synod.

Mission initiative roll

29A (1) Where a bishop's mission order is in force, the leader of the mission initiative must, at the direction of the bishop or bishops who made the order, establish and maintain a roll (a 'mission initiative roll') on which the names of lay persons are entered in accordance with this rule.

(2) If the mission initiative is represented on a deanery synod by virtue of a scheme under rule 27A, the bishop or bishops must give a direction under paragraph (1).

(3) A person is eligible to have the person's name on the roll if the person –

    (a) is baptised,

    (b) is aged 16 or over, and

    (c) has made a written application to have his or her name on the roll.

(4) An application under paragraph (3)(c) must include a declaration that the applicant –

    (a) either is a member of the Church of England or a Church in communion with it or is a member in good standing of a Church which is not in communion with the Church of England but which subscribes to the doctrine of the Holy Trinity, and

(b) has habitually attended public worship as part of the worshipping community involved in the initiative during the preceding six months.

(5) A person who is eligible to have the person's name on more than one mission initiative roll is entitled to have the person's name on each of the mission initiative rolls concerned.

(6) In the case of a mission initiative which is in more than one diocese, the function of giving a direction under paragraph (1) is exercisable by the diocesan bishops concerned acting jointly.

(7) A direction under paragraph (1) must be given on or before 15 September 2019; and where a direction under that paragraph is given –

(a) the function of establishing a mission initiative roll under that paragraph must be completed no later than 30 October 2019, and

(b) the leader of the mission initiative must, no later than 30 October 2019, give the secretary of the diocesan synod written notification of the number of names there are on the mission initiative roll as at the date on which the establishment of the roll was completed.

(8) In this rule, 'mission initiative' has the meaning given in Part 7 of the Mission and Pastoral Measure 2011 (and, where a mission initiative has more than one leader, a reference to the leader is to be read as a reference to any of them).

House of bishops

30 The members of the house of bishops of a diocesan synod are –

(a) the bishop of the diocese,

(b) each suffragan bishop of the diocese, and

(c) such other persons in episcopal orders who work in the diocese as the bishop of the diocese may nominate with the agreement of the archbishop of the province.

House of clergy

31 (1) The ex officio members of the house of clergy of a diocesan synod are –

(a) the dean of the cathedral church of the diocese or, where the diocese has more than one cathedral church, the dean of each of them,

(b) the archdeacon of each archdeaconry in the diocese,

(c) each proctor elected from the diocese or from a university or theological education institution in the diocese to the Lower House of Convocation of the province,

(d) any other member of the Lower House of Convocation of the province who resides in the diocese, being either an ex officio or co-opted member of that House or a person chosen by and from the clerical members of the religious communities in the province,

    (e) the chancellor of the diocese (if in Holy Orders),

    (f) the chair of the diocesan board of finance (if in Holy Orders),

    (g) the chair of the diocesan board of education (if in Holy Orders), and

    (h) the chair of the diocesan advisory committee (if in Holy Orders).

(2)   The other members of the house of clergy of a diocesan synod are –

    (a) any clerk in Holy Orders nominated by the bishop under Rule 33,

    (b) each person elected by the house of clergy of each deanery synod in the diocese in accordance with Rules 35 to 42, and

    (c) no more than five other persons, each of whom must be a clerk in Holy Orders and co-opted as a member by the house of clergy of the diocesan synod.

(3)   The reference in paragraph (1)(a) to the dean of the cathedral church of a diocese includes –

    (a) in the case of the diocese of London, a reference to the Dean of Westminster;

    (b) in the case of the diocese of Oxford, a reference to the Dean of Windsor;

    (c) in the case of the diocese of Winchester, a reference to the Deans of Jersey and Guernsey.

(4)   For the purposes of paragraph (1)(c) –

    (a) each institution which is a member of the University of London is to be treated as a separate university wholly in the diocese in which its main site is situated, and

    (b) any other university or theological education institution which is situated in more than one diocese is to be treated as being wholly in the diocese in which its main site is situated.

House of laity

32 (1)   The ex officio members of the house of laity of a diocesan synod are –

    (a) each person elected from the diocese as a member of the House of Laity of the General Synod,

    (b) any other member of the House of Laity of the General Synod who resides in the diocese, being either an ex officio or co-opted member of that House or a lay person chosen by and from the religious communities in the province,

(c) the chancellor of the diocese (if not in Holy Orders),

(d) the chair of the diocesan board of finance (if not in Holy Orders),

(e) the chair of the diocesan board of education (if not in Holy Orders), and

(f) the chair of the diocesan advisory committee (if not in Holy Orders).

(2) The other members of the house of laity of a diocesan synod are –

(a) any lay person nominated by the bishop under Rule 33,

(b) each person elected by the house of laity of each deanery synod in the diocese in accordance with Rules 35 to 42, and

(c) no more than five other persons, each of whom must be an actual communicant aged 16 or over and co-opted as a member by the house of laity of the diocesan synod.

Power of bishop to nominate members

33 (1) The bishop of a diocese may nominate up to ten additional members of the diocesan synod.

(2) A clerk in Holy Orders who is nominated under this Rule becomes a member of the house of clergy of the diocesan synod.

(3) A lay person who is nominated under this Rule becomes a member of the house of laity of the diocesan synod.

(4) A person who becomes a member of a diocesan synod under this Rule has the same rights, and is subject to the same requirements, as an elected member.

(5) Where a person nominated under this Rule is eligible under Rule 15 or 16 for membership of more than one deanery synod, the bishop's council and standing committee must designate the deanery synod of which the person is to be a member.

(6) Where a person nominated under this Rule is a lay person who is on the roll of more than one parish, the person must choose the PCC of which he or she is to be a member.

Restrictions on membership

34 (1) A person may not be a member of more than one diocesan synod at the same time unless the person is –

(a) the chancellor of the diocese, or

(b) if a parish in the diocese has passed a resolution under the House of Bishops' Declaration on the Ministry of Bishops and Priests of 19 May 2014, a suffragan bishop chosen by the bishop of the diocese to undertake ministry in respect of that parish.

(2) The registrar of a diocese and any deputy registrar are each disqualified from –

    (a) standing for election to the diocesan synod,

    (b) being nominated or co-opted as a member, and

    (c) being an ex officio member.

ELECTION OF MEMBERS

Timing

35 (1) Every three years beginning with 2021, the house of clergy and the house of laity of each deanery synod in a diocese must elect the members of the diocesan synod.

(2) The elections must be completed by 15 July; and accordingly the bishop of the diocese –

    (a) must fix the timetable and date for each election, and

    (b) must ensure that the secretary of each deanery synod is informed.

(3) An elected member holds office for a term of three years beginning with the next 1 August following the election.

Eligibility

36 (1) A clerk in Holy Orders who is a member of a deanery synod is qualified for election by the house of clergy of that deanery synod as a member of the diocesan synod.

(2) A clerk in Holy Orders may not stand for election by more than one deanery synod.

(3) A lay person is qualified for election by the house of laity of a deanery synod as a member of the diocesan synod if the person is an actual communicant aged 16 or over –

    (a) whose name is on the roll of a parish* in the deanery,

    (b) whose name is on the community roll of a cathedral church in the deanery which is not a parish church,

    (c) who, in a case where the area of the deanery includes Westminster

---

* A person whose name is on the roll of a guild church in the City of London is treated for this purpose as if his or her name is also on the roll of the parish in which the guild church is situated: see Rule 83(7) and (8).

Abbey, St George's Chapel, Windsor or the cathedral church of Christ in Oxford, is declared by the dean to be a habitual worshipper, or

(d) who is declared by the leader of a mission initiative in the deanery to be part of the worshipping community involved in the initiative.

(3A) The secretary of each diocesan synod shall, no later than 30 November 2019, certify to the Clerk to the General Synod the total number of names on mission initiative rolls (within the meaning given in rule 29A(8)) maintained in the diocese, as notified to the secretary under rule 29A(7)(b).

(3B) For the purposes of paragraph (3A), if a mission initiative is in more than one diocese, the number of names on the mission initiative roll for that initiative is to be divided equally between each diocese (but if it is not so divisible without remainder, the remainder is to be ignored); and the reference to the number of names on the mission initiative roll maintained in the diocese for that initiative is to be construed accordingly.

(4) A person whose name is on the roll of more than one parish must choose one of the parishes concerned for the purposes of paragraph (3)(a).

(5) A person who is part of the worshipping community involved in a mission initiative which is in more than one deanery, or who is part of the worshipping community involved in mission initiatives in different deaneries, must choose one of the deaneries concerned for the purposes of paragraph (3)(d).

Numbers

37 (1) A diocesan synod must, no later than 31 December in the year before an election of its members, determine for each house of each deanery synod in the diocese the number of members to be elected by that house.

(2) In the case of an election by the house of clergy of a deanery synod, the number of members to be elected –

(a) must relate to the number of members of the house, and

(b) must be at least two.

(3) In the case of an election by the house of laity of a deanery synod, the number of members to be elected –

(a) must relate to the number of names on the roll of each parish in the deanery as notified under Rule 10, and

(b) must be at least two.

(4) The secretary of each deanery synod must, no later than 1 July in the year before an election of the members of the diocesan synod, certify to the secretary of the diocesan synod the number of members of the house of clergy of that deanery synod as at 31 May.

(5) When exercising its functions under this Rule, a diocesan synod must act so as to ensure –

    (a) that the number of members of the synod is between 100 and 270, and

    (b) that the number of members of the house of clergy and the number of members of the house of laity are approximately equal.

(6) For the avoidance of doubt, the figure of 270 given in paragraph (5)(a) includes the maximum number of persons who may either be co-opted or be nominated by the bishop.

(7) The secretary of each diocesan synod must, no later than 31 December in the year before an election of its members, certify to the secretary of each deanery synod in the diocese the numbers determined under this Rule for each house of that synod.

Presiding officers

38 (1) The bishop of a diocese must appoint the presiding officers for an election of members of the diocesan synod.

(2) A person may not be appointed as a presiding officer for an election by a house of which that person is a member.

(3) The expenses of the elections are to be paid out of diocesan funds.

Qualified electors

39 (1) A person is a qualified elector in an election of members of a diocesan synod if the person's name and address is, as at 6.00 a.m. on the day on which nomination papers for the election are issued under Rule 40 –

    (a) in the case of an election by the house of clergy of a deanery synod in the diocese, recorded in the register of clerical electors, or

    (b) in the case of an election by the house of laity of a deanery synod in the diocese, recorded in the register of lay electors.

(2) But a member of either house who has been co-opted under Rule 18 is not a qualified elector in an election of members of the diocesan synod.

(3) The diocesan electoral registration officer must, at least 21 days before nomination papers are issued under Rule 40, give the secretary of each deanery synod in the diocese –

    (a) a copy of the names and addresses recorded in the register of clerical electors, and

    (b) a copy of those recorded in the register of lay electors.

(4) The secretary of each deanery synod must, within seven days of receiving the copy of the names and addresses, provide the diocesan electoral registration officer with –

   (a) if the names and addresses are correct, a certificate in writing to that effect, and

   (b) if they are not correct, a notification in writing of the corrections required.

(5) The diocesan electoral registration officer must, no later than seven days before nomination papers are issued under Rule 40, give a copy of the names and addresses (with whatever corrections are required having been made) to the presiding officer in the election.

(6) The register of clerical electors and the register of lay electors must be available for inspection at the diocesan office during the period beginning with the issue of nomination papers under Rule 40 and ending with the close of nominations.

(7) Each of the registers must, in the form in which it is made available for inspection, include the name of each elector but no other personal data.

(8) Corrections to either register may be made up until the close of nominations; but after the close of nominations, no names may be added to or removed from either register until the declaration of the result of the election.

Nomination

40 (1) A candidate for election to the house of clergy of a diocesan synod must be nominated by two qualified electors, each of whom is a member of the house of clergy of the deanery synod to which the candidate belongs.

   (2) A candidate for election to the house of laity of a diocesan synod must be nominated by two qualified electors, each of whom is a member of the house of laity of the deanery synod to which the candidate belongs.

   (3) The presiding officer for the election must ensure that each qualified elector is given a notice of election in Form 4 and a nomination paper in Form 5; and the manner in which the Forms are to be given is –

   (a) if the elector has notified the diocesan electoral registration officer that he or she wishes to use email for that purpose, by email to the address notified;

   (b) otherwise, by post to the address recorded for that elector in the register of clerical or lay electors or in person.

   (4) A nomination paper must be accompanied by a statement signed by the candidate –

(a) that he or she is willing to serve if elected, and

(b) if the candidate so wishes, setting out in no more than 100 words a factual statement for circulation with the voting papers of his or her professional qualifications, present office and relevant past experience.

(5) A nomination paper and the accompanying statement under paragraph (4) are to be given to the presiding officer; and the manner in which they are to be given is (subject to Rule 42(7)) –

(a) if the elector has notified the diocesan electoral registration officer that he or she wishes to use email for that purpose, by email from the address notified, with the nomination paper and accompanying statement each being in the form of a scanned copy of the original or such other electronic form as the presiding officer may authorise, or

(b) otherwise, by post or in person.

(6) The presiding officer must, in accordance with the timetable fixed by the bishop under Rule 35(2)(a), determine the period within which nomination papers and the accompanying statements are to be lodged with him or her; and the period so determined must be at least 21 days, subject to that timetable.

(7) Where a nomination paper or accompanying statement is sent by email, the presiding officer may require the elector to provide the original before the end of three days after the end of the period determined under paragraph (6).

(8) The presiding officer must –

(a) scrutinise each nomination paper as soon as it is lodged, and

(b) without delay, inform the candidate and each of the persons who nominated the candidate whether the nomination is valid.

(9) If the presiding officer rules that a nomination is not valid, the officer must give the candidate and each of the persons who nominated the candidate the reasons for the ruling when informing each of them of it under paragraph (8)(b) and give a written explanation of the right of appeal under Rule 58(1) against the ruling.

(10) A person is not included as a candidate for an election to a diocesan synod if the presiding officer has not received a valid nomination for that person –

(a) by the end of the period determined under paragraph (6), except in so far as there is a requirement under paragraph (7) to be complied with, and

(b) in so far as there is such a requirement, by the end of the three days referred to in that paragraph.

(11) The presiding officer must, within seven days of receiving a request from a validly nominated candidate, supply free of charge to that candidate one copy of the name and address of every qualified elector.

Requirement for election

41 (1) If the number of candidates for an election to a diocesan synod does not exceed the number of seats to be filled, each candidate is declared elected; and the presiding officer must inform each candidate and the secretary of the diocesan synod.

(2) If the number of candidates for an election to a diocesan synod exceeds the number of seats to be filled, an election must take place in accordance with Rule 42.

Conduct of election

42 (1) Where an election to a diocesan synod is to be held, the presiding officer for the election must ensure that each qualified elector is given a voting paper in Form 6, or is given a voting paper in Form 7, showing the name of each candidate; and the voting paper must be accompanied by a written explanation of the right of appeal under Rule 58(2) against the ruling that the nomination of a candidate is valid and of the right of appeal under Rule 58A against the result of the election.

(2) The diocesan synod must, no later than 31 December in the year before an election of its members, decide which form of voting paper is to be used by the deaneries in the election.

(3) Where an election to fill a casual vacancy is being conducted under this Rule by virtue of directions under Rule 45, the form of voting paper to be used is the form decided on under paragraph (2).

(4) A vote in an election to a diocesan synod is counted only if (subject to paragraph (5) and Rule 45(1) and (2)) it is given on a voting paper –

(a) which is marked in the manner indicated on the paper,

(b) the back of which is signed by the elector and has his or her full name and address written on it, and

(c) which is returned to the presiding officer within the period determined by him or her in accordance with the timetable fixed by the bishop under Rule 35(2)(a), with that period being at least 14 days, subject to that timetable.

(5) If there is a system of electronic voting for elections to the General Synod, a diocesan synod may itself resolve to have a system of electronic voting for elections to that synod; and, if a diocesan synod does so resolve, the elections to that synod must be conducted in accordance with rules which the General Synod has approved by resolution.

(6) Rules under paragraph (5) may make provision equivalent to that made under Rule 56 (election rules for the House of Laity of the General Synod) in relation

to electronic voting and may apply any provision of these Rules with or without modifications.

(7) If there is a system of electronic voting for elections to a diocesan synod, a completed nomination or voting paper may not be given by email; and Rule 76 (which makes provision authorising the use of email) is accordingly to be read subject to this paragraph.

(8) Where voting papers in Form 6 are used and there is an equality of votes, the presiding officer must decide the election by the drawing of a lot.

(9) An election in which voting papers in Form 7 are used is to be conducted by the single transferable vote system in accordance with the rules for the time being in force under the General Synod's Standing Orders, with whatever modifications to those rules are necessary.

(10) The presiding officer for an election to a diocesan synod must, no later than 1 August in the year in which the election is held, give a return of the result to –

(a) each candidate, and

(b) the secretary of the diocesan synod.

Scheme for variation of membership

43 (1) A diocesan synod may make a scheme to vary the preceding provisions of this Part of these Rules that relate to the membership of diocesan synods so as both –

(a) to meet the special circumstances of the diocese, and

(b) to secure better representation of clergy or of laity, or of both, on the diocesan synod.

(2) Where a scheme under this Rule has effect, the preceding provisions of this Part of these Rules, in so far as they apply to the diocesan synod in question, have effect subject to the scheme.

(3) A copy of a proposed scheme under this Rule must be given to members of the diocesan synod at least 14 days before the meeting at which it is to be considered for approval.

(4) A proposed scheme under this Rule is approved by the diocesan synod only if –

(a) the house of bishops approves it,

(b) in the house of clergy, it is approved by at least two-thirds of its members present and voting, and

(c) in the house of laity, it is approved by at least two-thirds of its members present and voting.

(5)   A proposed scheme under this Rule which is approved by the diocesan synod must be laid before the General Synod.

(6)   If a member of the General Synod gives notice in accordance with its Standing Orders that the member wishes a proposed scheme under this Rule to be debated, the scheme does not come into operation unless it is approved by the General Synod.

(7)   If a proposed scheme under this Rule is approved by the General Synod or no notice such as is mentioned in paragraph (6) is given, the scheme comes into operation –

(a)   on the day after the end of the group of sessions during which it was laid before, or approved by, the Synod, or

(b)   such later date as the scheme may specify.

Procedure

44   (1)   A diocesan synod must make standing orders.

(2)   The standing orders must include provision –

(a)   for the bishop of the diocese not to be required to chair meetings where the standing orders make other provision in that respect;

(b)   for a member of the house of clergy to be elected as chair of that house and a member of the house of laity to be elected as chair of that house;

(c)   for there to be a secretary;

(d)   for a specified number of meetings to be held each year, with the minimum being two;

(e)   for a meeting to be held if at least a specified number of members request that;

(f)   for the bishop of the diocese to have a second, casting vote where there is an equality of votes in the house of bishops;

(g)   for enabling the bishop of the diocese to require his or her opinion on a matter to be recorded in the minutes;

(h)   for there to be a bishop's council and standing committee of the synod which has such membership as the standing orders may provide and –

(i)   the functions exercisable by it under section 4 (4) of this Measure*, and

(ii)   such other functions as may be conferred by the standing orders or by or under this or any other Measure or by or under Canon.

(3)   The standing orders must also include provision –

---

*   i.e. the Synodical Government Measure 1969 of which these Rules form part.

(a) that, subject as follows, the assent of the synod is given only if each of the three houses gives its assent;

(b) that if the bishop of the diocese so directs on a question other than one on an Article 8 matter referred to the synod, the assent of the house of bishops is given only if the majority of the members who give assent includes the bishop;

(c) that a question relating only to the conduct of business is to be decided by the votes of the members present and voting;

(d) that any other question is to be decided by the votes of the members present and voting (with the assent of each of the three houses presumed), unless the bishop of the diocese or any ten members require there to be a separate vote by each house;

(e) that if the house of clergy and the house of laity are in favour of an Article 8 matter referred to the synod, it is deemed to be approved for the purposes of Article 8 of the Constitution.

(4) The standing orders may include provision for such other matters consistent with the provision required under paragraphs (2) and (3) as the diocesan synod decides.

(5) The provision which may be made under paragraph (4) includes provision to enable the chair of the house of clergy and the chair of the house of laity of the diocesan synod each to continue to hold office as such until the election of his or her successor as chair.

(6) A person may not serve as a member of more than one bishop's council and standing committee at the same time.

(7) The registrar of the diocese is the registrar of the diocesan synod.

(8) A reference in this Rule to an Article 8 matter referred to a diocesan synod is a reference to a matter referred by the General Synod to that diocesan synod under Article 8 of the Constitution.

Casual vacancies

45 (1) A casual vacancy* among the members of a diocesan synod elected by either house of a deanery synod may be filled by the election by that house of the deanery synod of a person qualified to be elected as such (as to which, see Rule 36).

(2) An election to fill a casual vacancy of that kind is to take place at a meeting of the members of that house of the deanery synod, unless the bishop of the diocese –

---

* 'Casual vacancy' includes the case where there is a vacancy because not enough candidates were nominated to fill the places available: see Rule 83(9).

    (a) directs that the election is to be conducted in accordance with Rules 38 to 42, and

    (b) fixes the timetable and date for the election accordingly and ensures that the secretary of the deanery synod is informed.

(3) An election to fill a casual vacancy of that kind is to be completed, so far as possible, within six months of the occurrence of the vacancy (subject to Rule 74).

(4) Where an election to fill a casual vacancy of that kind is to take place at a meeting under paragraph (2) but is not completed within six months of the occurrence of the vacancy, the bishop must give directions (which may include directions for the election to be conducted in accordance with Rules 38 to 42).

(5) Where an election to fill a casual vacancy is to take place by virtue of a direction of the bishop under paragraph (2)(a) or (4), Rules 38 to 42 have effect, but as if a reference to the timetable fixed under Rule 35(2)(a) were a reference to the timetable fixed under paragraph (2)(b) or by virtue of paragraph (4) of this Rule.

(6) Where the period for holding a general election to either house of a diocesan synod is due to begin within nine months of the occurrence of the vacancy, it is not to be filled unless the members of the bishop's council and standing committee who are from the house concerned direct otherwise.

PART 5

HOUSE OF LAITY OF THE GENERAL SYNOD

Membership

46 (1) The members of the House of Laity of the General Synod are –

    (a) each person elected by the diocesan electors of each diocese (see Rule 54),

    (b) each representative elected under the Channel Islands (Representation) Measure 1931,

    (c) two lay persons elected or chosen by and from the members of religious communities having their mother house in either province, with the election or choice being made in such manner as the rules under Rule 56 provide,

    (d) each person who is an ex officio member under Rule 47,

    (e) each person who is co-opted under Rule 48, and

    (f) at least three but no more than four other persons, each of whom is an actual communicant and who is elected or chosen as soon as practicable after a dissolution of the Synod in such manner as the Armed Forces Synod may decide or, in so far as provision is not made in that manner, in such manner as the rules under Rule 56 provide.

  (2) The term of office of a member of the House of Laity under paragraph (1)(a), (b), (c) or (f) is (subject to termination or resignation) for the lifetime of the Synod for which the member is elected or chosen; but that does not prevent the person from doing either of the following during a dissolution of the Synod –

    (a) acting under Article 3(4) of the Constitution (under which a person may continue to act as a member of a body of the Synod);

    (b) continuing to be an ex officio member of a body constituted under these Rules.

  (3) The deadline for qualifying as a member of a religious community for the purposes of paragraph (1)(c) is 6.00 a.m. on –

    (a) the date of the dissolution of the Synod, or

    (b) where there is a casual vacancy, the date on which nomination papers are issued.

(4) The total number of persons elected or chosen under the following provisions taken together must not exceed seven –

    (a) paragraph (1)(f) of this Rule,

    (b) in Canon H2 (representation of the clergy in the Lower House of the Convocations), paragraph 1(d) in the form which it takes in relation to the Province of Canterbury, and

    (c) in Canon H3 (constitution of the Upper Houses of the Convocations), paragraph 1(bb).

(5) For the purposes of this Part of these Rules, the diocese in Europe is to be treated as a diocese in the province of Canterbury.

Ex officio members

47 (1) Each of the following, if not in Holy Orders, is an ex officio member of the House of Laity –

    (a) the Dean of the Arches and Auditor;

    (b) the Vicar-General of the Province of Canterbury;

    (c) the Vicar-General of the Province of York;

    (d) each of the three Church Estates Commissioners;

    (e) the Chair of the Church of England Pensions Board;

    (f) each member of the Archbishops' Council who is an actual communicant;

    (g) the Chair of the Dioceses Commission.

(2) An ex officio member has the same rights and is subject to the same requirements as an elected member.

Co-option

48 (1) The House of Laity may co-opt a lay person aged 18 or over who is an actual communicant; but the number of co-opted members may not at any time exceed five.

(2) A person may be co-opted only if at least two-thirds of the Standing Committee of the House of Laity have consented, either at a meeting or in writing.

(3) A co-opted member has the same rights and is subject to the same requirements as an elected member.

(4) A co-opted member serves until the next dissolution of the Synod, subject to paragraph (5); but that does not prevent the member from doing either of the following during a dissolution of the Synod –

    (a) acting under Article 3(4) of the Constitution (under which a person may continue to act as a member of a body of the Synod);

(b) continuing to be an ex officio member of a body constituted under these Rules.

(5) The House of Laity may impose a shorter term of membership on a co-opted member than would otherwise be the case.

(6) Paragraphs (4) and (5) do not prevent a person from being co-opted on one or more subsequent occasions.

(7) The House of Laity may by standing orders make provision to regulate the procedure for the appointment of co-opted members and provision which is incidental to such appointments or which otherwise gives effect to this Rule.

Numbers

49 (1) The total number of the members of the House of Laity elected by the diocesan electors of each diocese ('directly elected members') and the representatives elected under the Channel Islands (Representation) Measure 1931 must not exceed 195.

(2) Each diocese must have at least three directly elected members, other than the diocese of Sodor and Man which is to elect only one member.

(3) The total number of directly elected members is to be decided by resolution of the General Synod no later than the last day of February in the fifth year after the most recent election of the House of Laity.

(4) A resolution under paragraph (3) must apportion the number of directly elected members between the province of Canterbury and the province of York –

(a) in the proportion of 70 to 30 (or as close to that as possible), or

(b) if the resolution specifies some other proportion, in that other proportion (or as close to it as possible).

(5) A resolution under paragraph (3) must divide the number of directly elected members among the dioceses so that the number of members to be elected by each diocese is as nearly as possible proportionate to the total of –

(a) the number of names on the rolls of the parishes in that diocese, and

(b) the number of names on the mission initiative rolls for mission initiatives in that diocese.

(6) The method for making the division required under paragraph (5) is to be specified by the Business Committee.

(7) The secretary of each diocesan synod must, no later than 1 August in the fourth year after the most recent election of the House of Laity, certify to the Clerk to the General Synod the total of –

(a) the number of the names on the rolls of the parishes in that diocese, as notified to the secretary under Rule 10, and

(b) the number of the names on the mission initiative rolls for the mission initiatives in the diocese, as notified to the secretary under Rule 27D.

(8) The number of directly elected members for a diocese must, once it has been decided by the General Synod, be certified as soon as is practicable to the secretary of the diocesan synod.

(9) If the General Synod is dissolved, or a dissolution is pending, but a resolution under paragraph (3) has not been made, the Presidents or the Synod may give directions as to deciding and certifying the number of directly elected members for each diocese.

(10) Directions under paragraph (9) may provide that the numbers decided and certified on the most recent occasion are to be treated as having been decided and certified for the purposes of the coming election.

(11) For the purposes of paragraphs (5)(b) and 7(b), if a mission initiative is in more than one diocese, the number of names on the mission initiative roll is to be divided equally between each diocese (but if it is not so divisible without remainder, the remainder is to be ignored); and the reference to the number of names on the mission initiative roll maintained in the diocese for that initiative is to be construed accordingly.

(12) The reference in paragraph (7)(b) to notifications under Rule 27D includes, in the case of any mission initiative roll established under Rule 29A of the Old Rules, a reference to the notification given under Rule paragraph (7)(b) of that Rule; and 'the Old Rules' has the meaning given in Rule 27A(7).

Qualifications for election

50 (1) A lay person is qualified for election for a diocese by the diocesan electors of that diocese if he or she meets –

(a) each of the first, second and third conditions, and

(b) one of the fourth, fifth and sixth conditions.

(2) The first condition is that the person has received Communion according to the use of the Church of England, or a Church in communion with it,* at least three times in the twelve months preceding the relevant day.

(3) The second condition is that the person –

(a) is confirmed or ready and desirous of being confirmed, or

---

*   A list of Churches in communion with the Church of England can be found in the Supplementary Material in the published version of the Canons of the Church of England (available in print from Church House Publishing or online at https://www.churchofengland.org/more/policy-and-thinking/canons-church-england).

    (b) comes within paragraph 1(b) of Canon B 15A (communicant member of Church which subscribes to doctrine of Holy Trinity).

(4) The third condition is that the person is aged 18 or over on the relevant day.

(5) The fourth condition is that the person's name is, as at 6.00 a.m. on the relevant day –

    (a) on the roll of a parish* in the diocese, or

    (b) in the case of a cathedral church which is not a parish church, on the community roll of the cathedral church.

(6) The fifth condition is that, in a case where the area of the diocese includes Westminster Abbey, St George's Chapel, Windsor or the cathedral church of Christ in Oxford, the person has at any time in the period of two months beginning one month before the relevant day, been declared by the dean to be a habitual worshipper.

(7) The sixth condition is that the person has, at any time in the period of two months beginning one month before the relevant day, been declared by the leader of a mission initiative in the diocese to be part of the worshipping community involved in the initiative.

(8) A person who is on the roll of more than one parish must choose one of those parishes for the purposes of this Rule.

(9) A person who is part of the worshipping community involved in a mission initiative which is in more than one diocese, or who is part of the worshipping community involved in mission initiatives in different dioceses, must choose one of the dioceses concerned for the purposes of this Rule.

(10) The 'relevant day' means –

    (a) the date of the dissolution of the Synod, or

    (b) in the case of an election to fill a casual vacancy, the date on which nomination papers are issued.

(11) Where a diocese is divided into two or more areas under Rule 51, a person who is qualified for election for that diocese –

    (a) may be a candidate for any one of those areas, regardless of whether the parish or cathedral church whose roll includes the person's name is in that area, but

    (b) may not be a candidate for more than one of those areas at the same time.

---

* A person whose name is on the roll of a guild church in the City of London is treated for this purpose as if his or her name is also on the roll of the parish in which the guild church is situated: see Rule 83(7) and (8).

Electoral areas

51 (1) Each diocese is an electoral area for the purposes of elections to the House of Laity, unless the diocese is divided into areas under this Rule.

(2) A diocesan synod may, for the purposes of an election to the House of Laity, divide the diocese into two or more areas and apportion between those areas the number of members to be elected for the diocese; and the number of members apportioned to each area must be at least three.

(3) But if elections to the House of Laity are conducted by the single transferable vote system provided for by rules for the time being in force under the General Synod's Standing Orders, the power under paragraph (2) may be exercised only so far as is consistent with those rules.

(4) Where a diocese is divided into areas under this Rule, the election in question is to be conducted in each of those areas as if it were a separate diocese.

(5) A division of a diocese under this Rule remains in force until it is revoked by the diocesan synod.

(6) Where a diocese is divided under this Rule –

(a) a diocesan elector who is a representative of the laity is entitled to vote in the area to which the body by which the elector was elected belongs;

(b) a diocesan elector who is not a representative of the laity is entitled to vote in whichever area the diocesan synod decides.

Timing

52 (1) The elections to the House of Laity are to be carried out in the period of three months immediately following a dissolution of the General Synod.

(2) The elections are to be carried out in each diocese during such part of that three-month period as the Presidents of the Synod jointly decide.

(3) This Rule has effect subject to any directions given by the General Synod or the Presidents.

Presiding officer

53 (1) For an election to the House of Laity, the presiding officer in each diocese or, where a diocese has been divided into areas under Rule 51, in each area of the diocese is –

(a) the registrar of the diocese or a person appointed by him or her with the approval of the registrar of the province, or

(b) if the registrar of the diocese is a candidate in the election, a person appointed by the registrar of the province.

(2)　The Business Committee must nominate an independent body which it is satisfied would be able to assist each presiding officer with the conduct of an election in the diocese to the House of Laity (including the issue of invitations to nominate and the lodging of nominations), in so far as the election involves a system of electronic voting.

(3)　The presiding officer of each diocese must appoint the body nominated under paragraph (2) and may not appoint any other body or any individual for that purpose.

(4)　The provincial registrars must jointly make rules imposing duties on the presiding officer in each diocese in connection with elections to the House of Laity held in that diocese.

(5)　Rules under paragraph (4) are of no effect unless the Business Committee has approved them.

Entitlement to vote

54　(1)　A person is entitled to vote in an election to the House of Laity held in a diocese if, at the close of nominations, the person is a diocesan elector in that diocese.

(2)　In each diocese other than the diocese in Europe, the diocesan electors are the members of the house of laity of each deanery synod in the diocese, apart from any person who is –

(a)　co-opted under Rule 18(2), or

(b)　a lay member of a religious community which has separate representation in the General Synod under Rule 46(1)(c).

(3)　In the diocese in Europe, the diocesan electors are the persons elected by the annual meeting of each chaplaincy, with the number to be elected being determined by the bishop's council and standing committee of the diocese; and a person is qualified for election as a diocesan elector if he or she is a lay person –

(a)　who is an actual communicant,

(b)　who is aged 18 or over, and

(c)　whose name is entered on the electoral roll of a chaplaincy in the diocese.

(4)　The deadline for qualifying as a diocesan elector in an election to the House of Laity is 6.00 a.m. on –

(a)　the date of the dissolution of the Synod, or

(b)　in the case of an election to fill a casual vacancy, the date on which invitations to nominate are issued.

(5)　The diocesan electoral registration officer must, at least 21 days before invitations to nominate are issued under Rule 55, give the secretary of each deanery synod in the diocese a copy of the names and addresses recorded in the register of lay electors.

(6) The secretary of each deanery synod must, within seven days of receiving the copy names and addresses, provide the diocesan electoral registration officer with –

    (a) if the names and addresses are correct, a certificate in writing to that effect, or

    (b) if they are not correct, a notification in writing of the corrections required.

(7) In ascertaining for the purposes of paragraph (6) whether the names and addresses are correct, the secretary of each deanery synod must ask each elector who has not provided an email address whether he or she wishes to provide one.

(8) The diocesan electoral registration officer must, no later than seven days before invitations to nominate are issued under Rule 55, give a copy of the names and addresses (with any corrections required having been made) to the presiding officer in the election.

(9) The register of lay electors must be available for inspection at the diocesan office during the period beginning with the issue of invitations to nominate under Rule 55 and ending with the close of nominations.

(10) The register of lay electors must, in the form in which it is made available for inspection, include the name of each elector but no other personal data.

(11) Corrections to the register may be made up until the close of nominations; but after the close of nominations, no names may be added to or removed from the register until the declaration of the result of the election.

Nomination

55 (1) A candidate for election in a diocese to the House of Laity must be nominated by two persons, each of whom is a diocesan elector in the diocese.

(2) The presiding officer in each diocese must ensure that each diocesan elector in the diocese is issued with an invitation to nominate.

(3) If a person who is qualified for election but is not a diocesan elector requests a nomination paper, the presiding officer must ensure that the person is issued with a nomination paper.

(4) The presiding officer must determine the period within which nominations are to be given to him or her; and the period so determined must be at least 28 days beginning with the day after that on which the invitations to nominate are issued.

(5)   The presiding officer must ensure that, when an invitation to nominate is issued to a person, the person is also given written notification of when nominations close.

Election rules

56 (1)   The General Synod must make rules relating to the conduct of an election to the House of Laity (including an election to fill a casual vacancy).*

(2)   The rules may, in particular, make provision as to –

(a)   the system by which, and the manner in which, the election is to be conducted;

(b)   the process for issuing invitations to nominate and for the lodging and scrutiny of nominations;

(c)   the conditions for the validity of a nomination;

(d)   the preparation, circulation and distribution of election addresses and other election papers;

(e)   the conditions for the validity of a vote in the election;

(f)   the functions which the presiding officer is required or authorised to carry out in connection with the election;

(g)   the assistance which the body nominated under Rule 53(2) may provide to a presiding officer;

(h)   the entitlement of a presiding officer to a fee for the exercise of a function in connection with the election and the entitlement of the body nominated under Rule 53(2) to a fee for the assistance it provides to a presiding officer;

(i)   the liability to pay the expenses of the election.

(3)   The rules may, in so far as they provide for an election to the House of Laity to involve a system of electronic voting, modify the application of any provision of these Rules.

(4)   The rules may –

(a)   make different provision for different cases;

(b)   make provision which applies generally or for specified cases or subject to specified exceptions;

(c)   make supplementary, transitional or saving provision;

(d)   make provision which confers a discretion on a person.

(5)   The rules are to be made in accordance with the Standing Orders of the General Synod.

---

*   These rules have now been made by the General Synod and are on the Church of England website.

PART 6

APPEALS

Enrolment appeals

57 (1) A person who is refused enrolment on the roll of a parish or the register of clerical or lay electors may appeal against the refusal.

(2) A person whose name is removed from the roll of a parish or the register of clerical or lay electors may appeal against the removal.

(3) A person whose name is entered on the roll of a parish or the register of clerical or lay electors and who objects to the enrolment of another person on, or to the removal of another person's name from, the roll or register may appeal against the enrolment or removal.

(4) Notice of an appeal under this Rule –

(a) must be in writing,

(b) must give brief particulars of the grounds of the appeal, and

(c) may be accompanied by written submissions.

(5) Notice of an appeal under this Rule relating to the roll of a parish must be given to the lay chair of the deanery synod.

(6) Notice of an appeal under this Rule relating to the register of lay electors must be given to the chair of the house of laity of the diocesan synod.

(7) Notice of an appeal under this Rule relating to the register of clerical electors must be given to the chair of the house of clergy of the diocesan synod.

(8) Notice of an appeal under this Rule must be given no later than 14 days after –

(a) the date of the notification of the refusal, removal or enrolment concerned,

(b) if the appeal arises from a revision of the roll of a parish or the creation of a new roll for a parish, the day on which the revised or new roll is published under Rule 5 or 8, or

(c) if the appeal arises from the creation or revision of a register of clerical or lay electors, the end of the period for which the register is made available for inspection under Rule 39(6).

Enrolment appeals: referral and representations etc.

57A (1) Where notice of an appeal under Rule 57 is given, the person to whom it is given must without delay (and in any event within 48 hours of receiving it unless the appellant has in the meantime given written notice to withdraw the appeal) –

    (a) refer the notice to the bishop's council and standing committee,

    (b) in the case of an appeal under Rule 57(3), give a written notification to the person to whose enrolment or removal from the roll or register the objection is made, and

    (c) give a written notification to each person who made a decision to which the appeal relates.

(2) Where a purported notice of an appeal under Rule 57 is given out of time, the person to whom it is given must without delay (and in any event within 48 hours of receiving it unless the appellant has in the meantime given written notice to withdraw the appeal) –

    (a) refer the purported notice of appeal to the bishop's council and standing committee, and

    (b) give a written notification to each person referred to in paragraph (1)(b) and (c).

(3) An appeal under Rule 57 is to be dealt with in accordance with Rules 61B to 61G and 61I.

(4) A person to whom a notification is given under paragraph (1)(b) is entitled to make written representations to the panel appointed under Rule 61C(1) on a decision to which the appeal relates.

(5) A person to whom a notification is given under paragraph (1)(c) is entitled to provide that panel with a written explanation of the reasons for the decision which that person made.

(6) Representations under paragraph (4) or an explanation under paragraph (5) must be made within 28 days of referral of the notice of appeal.

(7) A person to whom a notification is given under paragraph (2)(b) is entitled to make written representations to the panel appointed under Rule 61C(2) on the question of whether the panel should consider the appeal.

(8) Representations under paragraph (7) must be made within seven days of the notification under paragraph (2)(b) being given.

(9) A notification under paragraph (1)(b) or (c) or (2)(b) must include an explanation of the entitlement to make representations or an explanation (as the case may be).

(10) A reference in this Part to an 'enrolment appeal' is a reference to an appeal under Rule 57.

Nomination appeals

58 (1) An appeal may be made against a determination that a nomination of a candidate for a relevant election is not valid on the grounds that the nomination is valid and that the person should, accordingly, be included as a candidate for the election.

(2) An appeal may be made against a determination that a nomination of a candidate for a relevant election is valid on the grounds that the nomination is not valid and that the person should, accordingly, not be included as a candidate for the election.

(3) An appeal under paragraph (1) or (2) may be brought only by an elector in the election.

(4) In this Rule, 'relevant election' –

(a) means an election under these Rules or to a body constituted in accordance with these Rules, but

(b) does not include an election to the House of Laity of the General Synod.

(5) In a case where a choice of persons is, or is to be, made under these Rules (rather than an election being held), this Rule and the subsequent Rules in this Part apply to the choice as they apply to an election; and the references to elections are to be read accordingly.

Election appeals

58A (1) An appeal may be made against the result of a relevant election on the grounds that a person whose election is the subject of the appeal –

(a) was not duly elected,

(b) was not qualified to be a candidate at the time of the election, or

(c) before the end of the period for voting, misrepresented a material fact in connection with the election.

(2) An appeal may be made against the result of a relevant election on the grounds that the conduct of the election was such as to affect the outcome of the election.

(3) An appeal may be made against the result of a relevant election on the grounds that –

(a) it has been determined on an enrolment appeal that an error was made in the roll of a parish or the register of clerical or lay electors or the question is awaiting determination on an enrolment appeal, and

(b) the error would or might be material to the result of the election.

(4) An appeal may be made against the result of a relevant election on the grounds that a vote which was allowed should have been disallowed, or that a vote which was disallowed should have been allowed, but only if the allowance or disallowance of the vote would or might be material to the result of the election.

(5) An appeal may not be brought under paragraph (1)(b) if –

(a) the grounds of the appeal are to the effect that the nomination of the person whose election is the subject of the appeal was not valid, and

(b) an appeal on grounds to that effect was brought under Rule 58(2) before the election.

(6) An appeal under this Rule may be brought by –

(a) a candidate in the election,

(b) a person entitled to vote in the election, or

(c) the chair of the house of laity of the diocesan synod (where the appeal relates to laity) or the chair of the house of clergy (where the appeal relates to clergy).

(7) On an appeal under this Rule, a person who was declared elected but whose election is or may be affected by the appeal is to be regarded for all purposes as elected pending the determination of the appeal.

(8) In this Rule, 'relevant election' –

(a) means an election held (or purporting to be held) under these Rules or an election to a body constituted in accordance with these Rules, but

(b) does not include an election to the House of Laity of the General Synod.

Election appeals: power to make rules for House of Laity of General Synod

59 (1) The General Synod must make rules providing for –

(a) a right of appeal relating to a person's eligibility to vote in an election to the House of Laity of the General Synod for the purposes of Rule 46(1)(c) or (f) (religious communities and Armed Forces Synod);

(b) a right of appeal against a determination of whether a nomination of a candidate for election to that House is valid;

(c) a right of appeal against the result of an election to that House.*

---

* These rules have now been made by the General Synod and are on the Church of England website.

(2) The rules may provide that, on an appeal arising out of an election to the House of Laity, a person who was declared elected but whose election is or may be affected by the appeal is to be regarded for all purposes as a member of that House pending the determination of the appeal.

(2A) The rules may include provision as to the payment of expenses incurred by the person who determines an appeal under the rules.

(3) The rules may –

(a) make different provision for different cases;

(b) make provision which applies generally or for specified cases or subject to specified exceptions;

(c) make supplementary, transitional or saving provision;

(d) make provision which confers a discretion on a person.

(4) The rules may apply a provision of this Part of these Rules with or without modifications.

(5) The rules are to be made in accordance with the Standing Orders of the General Synod.

Election appeals: appeal procedures

59A (1) Each of the following appeals (referred to in this Part as a 'summary election appeal') is to be dealt with in accordance with Rules 60 to 60C and 61I –

(a) an appeal under Rule 58(1) or (2) (validity of nomination);

(b) an appeal under Rule 58A(1)(a) or (b) (whether person duly elected or qualified to be candidate);

(c) an appeal under Rule 58A(4) (allowance or disallowance of vote).

(2) Each of the following appeals (referred to in this Part as a 'full election appeal') is to be dealt with in accordance with Rules 61 to 61F, 61H and 61I –

(a) an appeal under Rule 58A(1)(c) (misrepresentation of material fact);

(b) an appeal under Rule 58A(2) (conduct of election);

(c) an appeal under Rule 58A(3) (error in church electoral roll or register of clerical or lay electors).

Summary election appeal: notice

60 (1) Notice of a summary election appeal –

(a) must be in writing,

(b) must give brief particulars of the grounds of appeal, and

(c) may be accompanied by written submissions.

(2) Notice of a summary election appeal must be given to the presiding officer for the election.

(3) Notice of an appeal under Rule 58(1) (appeal against ruling that nomination not valid) must be given no later than two days after the day on which the person to whom the nomination relates is notified of the ruling that the nomination is not valid.

(4) Notice of an appeal under Rule 58(2) (appeal against ruling that nomination valid) brought by a person entitled to vote in the election (including one who is a candidate) must be given no later than two days after the day on which the person receives a voting paper for the election.

(5) Notice of an appeal under Rule 58A(1)(a) or (b) (appeal relating to whether person duly elected or qualified to be candidate) must be given no later than two days after the day on which the result of the election is declared.

(6) Notice of an appeal under Rule 58A(4) (appeal against allowance or disallowance of vote) must be given no later than two days after –

(a) the day on which the vote in question is allowed or disallowed, or

(b) if the appeal is being brought on grounds that there is an error in the roll of a parish or the register of clerical or lay electors but an enrolment appeal has yet to be determined, the day on which that appeal is determined.

Summary election appeal: referral to relevant judge, etc.

60A (1) The presiding officer for an election, having received notice of a summary election appeal, must without delay (and in any event within 48 hours of receiving the notice of appeal unless in the meantime written notice is given to withdraw the appeal) –

(a) refer the notice of appeal to the relevant judge,

(b) give a written notification to each candidate in the election,

(c) if any decision to which the appeal relates was made by a person other than the presiding officer, give a written notification to that person, and

(d) in the case of an appeal under Rule 58(1) or (2), give a written notification to the person whose nomination is the subject of the appeal.

(2) A person to whom a notification is given under paragraph (1)(b) or (d) is entitled to make written representations to the relevant judge on a decision to which the appeal relates.

(3) The presiding officer is entitled to provide the relevant judge with a written explanation of the reasons for any decision made by the officer to which the appeal relates.

(4) A person to whom a notification is given under paragraph (1)(c) is entitled to provide the relevant judge with a written explanation of the reasons for the decision which that person made.

(5) Representations under paragraph (2) or an explanation under paragraph (3) or (4) must be made within seven days of the referral of the notice of appeal.

(6) A notification under paragraph (1)(b), (c) or (d) must include an explanation of the entitlement to make representations or an explanation (as the case may be).

(7) The 'relevant judge' is –

(a) the Dean of the Arches and Auditor, or

(b) if the Dean of the Arches and Auditor declines or is unable to act as such, the Vicar-General of the Province of Canterbury or the Vicar-General of the Province of York, or

(c) if each of them declines or is unable to act as such, the chancellor of the diocese concerned.

Summary election appeal: parties

60B (1) On a summary election appeal, each of the following is a party to the appeal (in addition to the appellant) –

(a) the presiding officer;

(b) any person to whom a notification is given under Rule 60A(1)(c);

(c) each relevant person.

(2) Each of the following is a relevant person –

(a) on an appeal under Rule 58(1) or (2), the person whose nomination is the subject of the appeal;

(b) on an appeal under Rule 58A(1)(a) or (b), the person whose election is the subject of the appeal;

(c) on an appeal under Rule 58A(4), any person to whom a notification is given under Rule 60A(1)(b).

Summary election appeal: determination

60C (1) The relevant judge (referred to in this Rule as 'the judge'), having had a notice of appeal referred under Rule 60A(1), must decide whether the grounds of the appeal are established to the judge's satisfaction.

(2) The judge, in deciding the matter at issue, may consider only –

(a) the notice of appeal and any accompanying written submissions, and

(b) any representations or explanation made in accordance with Rule 60A(5).

(3)   A decision under this Rule must be made within seven days of the referral of the notice of appeal.

(4)   Where the judge decides on an appeal under Rule 58(1) that a nomination is valid, or decides on an appeal under Rule 58(2) that a nomination is not valid, the judge must –

(a) give directions for the appointment of a new period for voting in the election, and

(b) give whatever further directions the judge thinks necessary.

(5)   Where, on an appeal under Rule 58A(1)(a) or (b) or (4), the judge decides that the election as a whole is void, the judge must –

(a) direct that a fresh election is to be held, and

(b) give whatever further directions the judge thinks necessary.

(6)   Where, on an appeal under Rule 58A(1)(a) or (b) or (4), the judge allows the appeal but does not decide that the election as a whole is void, the judge must give whatever directions the judge thinks necessary.

(7)   The judge on a summary appeal must otherwise decide one of the following –

(a) that the matter at issue amounts to a minor infringement which did not affect the outcome of the election and the appeal should accordingly be dismissed;

(b) that the matter at issue amounts to a procedural irregularity in the conduct of the election but the appeal should nonetheless in all the circumstances be dismissed;

(c) that the appeal is wholly without merit and should accordingly be dismissed.

Full election appeal: notice of appeal

61   (1)   Notice of a full election appeal –

(a) must be in writing,

(b) must give brief particulars of the grounds of appeal, and

(c) may be accompanied by written submissions.

(2)   Notice of a full election appeal must be given to the presiding officer for the election.

(3)   Notice of an appeal under Rule 58A(1)(c) or (2) must be given no later than 14 days after the day on which the result of the election is declared.

(4)   Notice of an appeal under Rule 58A(3) must be given no later than 14 days after –

(a) the day on which the result of the election is declared, or

(b) if an enrolment appeal has yet to be determined, the day on which that appeal is determined.

Full election appeal: referral to bishop's council and standing committee

61A (1) Where notice of a full election appeal is given, the person to whom it is given must without delay (and in any event within 48 hours of receiving it unless in the meantime written notice is given to withdraw the appeal) –

(a) give a written notification to each candidate in the election,

(b) if any decision to which the appeal relates was made by a person other than the presiding officer, give a written notification to that person, and

(c) refer the notice to the bishop's council and standing committee.

(2) Where a purported notice of a full election appeal is given out of time, the person to whom it is given must without delay (and in any event within 48 hours of receiving it unless in the meantime written notice is given to withdraw the appeal) –

(a) give a written notification to each person referred to in paragraph (1)(a) and (b), and

(b) refer the purported notice to the bishop's council and standing committee.

(3) A person to whom a notification is given under paragraph (1)(a) is entitled to make written representations to the panel appointed under Rule 61C(1) on a decision to which the appeal relates.

(4) The presiding officer is entitled to provide that panel with a written explanation of the reasons for any decision made by the officer to which the appeal relates.

(5) A person to whom a notification is given under paragraph (1)(b) is entitled to provide that panel with a written explanation of the reasons for the decision which that person made.

(6) Representations under paragraph (3) or an explanation under paragraph (4) or (5) must be made within 28 days of referral of the notice of appeal.

(7) The presiding officer and any person to whom a notification is given under paragraph (2)(a) are each entitled to make written representations to the panel appointed under Rule 61C(2) on the question of whether the panel should consider the appeal.

(8) Representations under paragraph (7) must be made within seven days of the notification under paragraph (2)(a) being given.

(9) A notification under paragraph (1)(a) or (b) or (2)(a) must include an explanation of the entitlement to make representations or an explanation (as the case may be).

(10) Once a notice is referred under this Rule, the appellant may withdraw it only with the consent of the panel appointed under Rule 61C to decide the matter.

Enrolment appeal or full election appeal: parties

61B (1) On an enrolment appeal, each of the following is a party to the appeal (in addition to the appellant) –

(a) the person to whom the notice of appeal is given;

(b) any person to whom a notification is given under Rule 57A(1)(c);

(c) on any appeal under Rule 57(3), the person to whose enrolment or removal from the roll or register the objection is made.

(2) On a full election appeal, each of the following is a party to the appeal (in addition to the appellant) –

(a) the presiding officer;

(b) any person to whom a notification is given under Rule 61A(1)(b);

(c) each relevant person.

(3) Each of the following is a relevant person –

(a) on an appeal under Rule 58A(1)(c), the person whose election is the subject of the appeal;

(b) on an appeal under Rule 58A(2) or (3), any person to whom a notification is given under Rule 61A(1)(a).

Enrolment appeal or full election appeal: appointment of panel

61C (1) The bishop's council and standing committee, on receiving a referral under Rule 57A(1) or 61A(1), must appoint a Chair and two other persons to serve as a panel to consider the appeal.

(2) The bishop's council and standing committee, on receiving a referral under Rule 57A(2) or 61A(2), must appoint a Chair and two other persons to serve as a panel to decide whether, even though the purported notice of appeal was given out of time, the panel will nonetheless consider the appeal.

(3) In making the appointments under this Rule, the bishop's council and standing committee must be satisfied that the persons appointed, taken together, have suitable legal or other experience or expertise.

(4) A person may not be appointed under this Rule if the person might have a benefit from the outcome of the election.

(5) Appointments under this Rule must be made before the end of 28 days beginning with the day on which the notice of appeal is given under Rule 57 or 61.

Enrolment appeal or full election appeal: preliminary assessment

61D (1) A panel appointed under Rule 61C(1) must conduct a preliminary assessment of the appeal.

(2) A preliminary assessment of an appeal is an assessment as to whether there are arguable grounds of appeal; and, in conducting a preliminary assessment, the panel may consider only –

(a) the notice of appeal and any accompanying written submissions, and

(b) any representations or explanation made in accordance with Rule 57A(6) or 61A(6).

(3) If the panel considers that there are arguable grounds of appeal, the appeal stands referred to the panel for –

(a) in the case of an enrolment appeal, consideration and determination under Rules 61F and 61G;

(b) in the case of a full election appeal, consideration and determination under Rules 61F and 61H.

(4) If the panel considers that there are no arguable grounds of appeal, the appeal is dismissed.

(5) The panel's decision on the preliminary assessment is final.

(6) The panel must give a written notification to the parties to the appeal of the decision on the preliminary assessment of the appeal and the reasons for the decision.

Enrolment appeal or full election appeal: appeal out of time

61E (1) A panel appointed under Rule 61C(2) may decide to consider the appeal only if, having regard to all the circumstances, it is satisfied that there is a good reason to allow the appeal to proceed.

(2) The matters which the panel considers in making that decision must include –

(a) the purported notice of appeal and any accompanying written submissions (whether on the question of why notice of appeal was not given within the required period or on any other point), and

(b) any representations made in accordance with Rule 57A(8) or 61A(8).

(3) Where the panel decides to consider the appeal –

(a) the period under Rule 57 or 61 for giving notice of appeal in that case is to be treated as having been extended so far as necessary,

(b) the appeal is to be treated as having been referred to the panel for decision, and

(c) the panel must ensure that each notification required under Rule 57A(1)(b) or (c) or 61A(a) or (b) is given to the person concerned (and, once that has been done, Rule 57A(4) to (6) and (9) or Rule 61A(3) to (6) and (9) applies in relation to the notification).

(4) Where the panel has decided to consider the appeal and the period for making representations in accordance with Rule 57A(6) or 61A(6) has expired, the panel may proceed to conduct a preliminary assessment of the appeal under Rule 61D.

(5) The panel must give a written notification to the parties to the appeal of the decision on whether the panel will consider the appeal and the reasons for the decision.

Enrolment appeal or full election appeal: consideration of matters at issue

61F (1) The panel to which an enrolment appeal or a full election appeal is referred must, in deciding the matter at issue, consider all the circumstances; and for that purpose the panel –

(a) may inspect documents or other papers relating to the subject-matter of the appeal, and

(b) is entitled to be provided with such information relating to the appeal as the panel may require.

(2) The panel must give each party to the appeal an opportunity –

(a) to appear before the panel in person or by a legal or other representative, or

(b) if that party does not wish to take that opportunity, to make written representations on the matter at issue.

(3) A hearing under paragraph (2) is to be held in public unless the panel, having regard to all the circumstances, is satisfied that it would be in the interests of justice for the hearing to be held in private.

Enrolment appeal: determination

61G (1) On an enrolment appeal, the panel must decide whether the grounds of appeal are established to the panel's satisfaction.

(2) Where the panel allows the appeal, it must –

(a) direct that the roll of the parish or the register of clerical or lay electors is to be revised as the panel specifies, and

(b) give whatever further directions the panel thinks necessary.

Full election appeal: determination

61H (1) On a full election appeal, the panel must decide whether the grounds of appeal are established to the panel's satisfaction.

(2) Where the panel decides that the election as a whole is void, it must –

(a) direct that a fresh election is to be held, and

(b) give whatever further directions the panel thinks necessary.

(3) Where the panel allows the appeal but does not decide that the election as a whole is void, it must give whatever directions it thinks necessary.

(4) The panel on a full election appeal must otherwise decide one of the following –

(a) that the matter at issue amounts to a minor infringement which did not affect the outcome of the election and the appeal should accordingly be dismissed;

(b) that the matter at issue amounts to a procedural irregularity in the conduct of the election but the appeal should nonetheless in all the circumstances be dismissed;

(c) that the appeal is wholly without merit and should accordingly be dismissed.

Appeals: general

61I (1) The decision on an appeal under this Part is final as to the matters at issue.

(2) The relevant judge or the panel which made the decision on an appeal under this Part must give a written notification to the parties to the appeal of the decision and the reasons for the decision.

(3) Where the direction that a fresh election is to be held is given under Rule 60C(5)(a) or 61H(2)(a), the date on which the direction is given is the date on which a casual vacancy occurs for the purposes of these Rules.

(4) The relevant judge or the panel on an appeal under this Part may direct that a party to the appeal must pay the whole or part of the expenses of the relevant judge or the panel; and a direction under this paragraph must specify the amount which the party must pay.

(5) The diocesan board of finance must pay the reasonable expenses of the relevant judge or the panel, in so far as they are not paid under paragraph (4).

PART 7

DISQUALIFICATION ETC.

Disqualifications

62 (1) A person is disqualified from being nominated or elected or from serving as a member of the General Synod if the person holds or takes a paid office or employment the appointment to which is, or may be, made or confirmed by –

(a) the General Synod,

(b) the Convocations,

(c) the Archbishops' Council,

(d) the Church Commissioners,

(e) the Church of England Pensions Board, or

(f) the Corporation of the Church House.

(2) A person is not disqualified under paragraph (1)(d) merely because the person is appointed as a Church Commissioner in receipt of a salary or other emoluments.

(3) A person is disqualified from being nominated, chosen or elected or from serving as a member of a PCC if the person has been disqualified from holding office under section 10(6) of the Incumbents (Vacation of Benefices) Measure 1977 (breakdown of pastoral relationships).

(4) Nothing in this Part of these Rules, so far as relating to membership of a PCC, affects the application of any enactment providing for the disqualification of a person from being a trustee of a charity* (and, accordingly, from being a member of a PCC).

(5) For further provision as to disqualification, see Rule 68 (safeguarding).

(6) For provision as to disqualification from being elected as a churchwarden, see section 2 of the Churchwardens Measure 2001.

Vacation of seat on deanery synod

63 (1) The seat of a clerical member of a deanery synod who is a member under sub-paragraph (a) to (f) or (h) of Rule 15(1) is vacated if the member ceases to be eligible for membership under that sub-paragraph and is not eligible for membership under another sub-paragraph of Rule 15(1).

---

* See Part 9 of the Charities Act 2011 (available at http://www.legislation.gov.uk/).

(2) The seat of a lay member of a deanery synod is vacated in each of the following five cases.

(3) The first case is where the member –

(a) was elected as a parochial representative of the laity, but

(b) ceases to have his or her name on the roll of the parish by which he or she was elected.

(4) The second case is where the member –

(a) became a representative under Rule 23(1) (cathedral church), but

(b) ceases to have his or her name on the community roll of the cathedral church concerned.

(5) The third case is where the member –

(a) became a representative under a scheme under Rule 23(2) (royal peculiar etc.), but

(b) ceases to be declared by the dean concerned to be a habitual worshipper.

(6) The fourth case is where the member –

(a) became a representative under a scheme under Rule 24 (mission initiative), but

(b) ceases to be declared by the leader of the mission initiative concerned to be part of the worshipping community involved in the initiative.

(7) The fifth case is where the member becomes a clerk in Holy Orders.

(8) A lay member's seat is not vacated under paragraph (3) if –

(a) the member satisfies a condition under paragraph (9), and

(b) before the vacancy arises, the PCC resolves that the member's seat is not to be vacated.

(9) The conditions are as follows –

(a) that the member's name is entered on the roll of a parish* in the diocese;

(b) that the member's name is entered on the community roll of the cathedral church of the diocese or, where the diocese has more than one cathedral church, on the community roll of any of them;

(c) that the leader of a mission initiative in the diocese declares the member to be part of the worshipping community involved in the initiative.

(10) A member's seat on a deanery synod is vacated if it is decided on an appeal under Rule 58 that the member's election is void.

---

* A person whose name is on the roll of a guild church in the City of London is treated for this purpose as if his or her name is also on the roll of the parish in which the guild church is situated: see Rule 83(7) and (8).

(11) For further cases where a member's seat on a deanery synod is vacated, see Rule 68 (safeguarding etc.).

Vacation of seat on diocesan synod

64 (1) The seat of a clerical member of a diocesan synod who was elected by the house of clergy of a deanery synod in the diocese is vacated if the member ceases to be qualified for election by that house.

(2) But a member's seat is not vacated under paragraph (1) if –

(a) the member continues to work or reside in the diocese, and

(b) before the vacancy arises, the clerical members of the standing committee of the deanery synod resolve that the member's seat is not to be vacated.

(3) The seat of a lay member of a diocesan synod who was elected by the house of laity of a deanery synod in the diocese is vacated in each of the following five cases.

(4) The first case is where the member –

(a) qualified for election under Rule 36(3)(a) (parish roll), but

(b) ceases to have his or her name on the roll of a parish in the deanery.

(5) The second case is where the member –

(a) qualified for election under Rule 36(3)(b) (cathedral church), but

(b) ceases to have his or her name on the community roll of the cathedral church concerned.

(6) The third case is where the member –

(a) qualified for election under Rule 36(3)(c) (royal peculiar etc.), but

(b) ceases to be declared by the dean to be a habitual worshipper.

(7) The fourth case is where the member –

(a) qualified for election under Rule 36(3)(d) (mission initiative), but

(b) ceases to be declared by the leader of the mission initiative concerned to be part of the worshipping community involved in the initiative.

(8) The fifth case is where the member becomes a clerk in Holy Orders.

(9) A lay member's seat is not vacated under paragraph (4) if –

(a) the member satisfies a condition in Rule 63(9), and

(b) before the vacancy arises, the lay members of the standing committee of the deanery synod resolve that the member's seat is not to be vacated.

(10) If a lay member of a diocesan synod is also an elected member of the House of Laity of the General Synod, the member's seat on the diocesan synod is

not vacated under this Rule if the bishop's council and standing committee make the decision referred to in Rule 65(7) (member willing and able to serve) in that member's case.

(11) A member's seat on a diocesan synod is vacated if it is decided on an appeal under Rule 58 that the member's election is void.

(12) For further cases where a member's seat on a diocesan synod is vacated, see Rule 68 (safeguarding etc.).

Vacation of seat in House of Laity of General Synod

65 (1) The seat of an elected member of the House of Laity of the General Synod is vacated in each of the following five cases.

(2) The first case is where the member –

    (a) qualified for election under Rule 50(5)(a) (parish roll), but

    (b) ceases to have his or her name on the roll of a parish in the diocese concerned.

(3) The second case is where the member –

    (a) qualified for election under Rule 50(5)(b) (cathedral church), but

    (b) ceases to have his or her name on the community roll of the cathedral church of the diocese or, where the diocese has more than one cathedral church, on the community roll of any of them.

(4) The third case is where the member –

    (a) qualified for election under Rule 50(6) (royal peculiar etc.), but

    (b) ceases to be declared by the dean concerned to be a habitual worshipper.

(5) The fourth case is where the member –

    (a) qualified for election under Rule 50(7) (mission initiative), but

    (b) ceases to be declared by the leader of the mission initiative concerned to be part of the worshipping community involved in the initiative.

(6) The fifth case is where the member becomes a clerk in Holy Orders.

(7) But a member's seat is not vacated under paragraphs (2) to (5) if, before the vacancy arises, the lay members of the bishop's council and standing committee decide that the member is willing and able to discharge to their satisfaction the duties of a member of the House of Laity of the General Synod elected for that diocese.

(8) Where a decision under paragraph (7) is made, the lay members of the bishop's council and standing committee must, no later than one year after making the decision and annually after that –

    (a) review the member's membership of the House of Laity of the General Synod, and

     (b) decide whether he or she is still willing and able as mentioned in paragraph (7).

(9)   The seat of an elected member of the House of Laity of the General Synod is vacated if the member is disqualified under Rule 62(1).

(10) The seat of an elected member of the House of Laity of the General Synod is vacated if it is decided on an appeal under rules under Rule 59 that the member's election is void.

(11) For further cases where a member's seat in the House of Laity of the General Synod is vacated, see Rule 68 (safeguarding etc.).

Ex officio membership

66 (1) A person is not disqualified from being elected or chosen as a member of a body under these Rules merely because the person is also a member of that body ex officio.

     (2) A person elected or chosen as a member of a body under these Rules does not vacate his or her seat merely because the person has become a member of that body ex officio.

Resignation

67 (1) A person holding office under these Rules or who is a member of a body constituted by or under these Rules may resign the office or membership by giving notice in writing to the secretary of the body of which the person is an officer or member.

     (2) A resignation under this Rule takes effect –

     (a) on the date specified in the notice, or

     (b) if no date is specified in the notice, on the date on which the secretary receives the notice.

Safeguarding cases: disqualification and vacation of seat

68 (1) If a person is included in a barred list, the person is disqualified –

     (a) from being nominated, chosen or elected as, or from serving as, a member of a PCC, a deanery synod, a diocesan synod or the General Synod;

     (b) from being appointed to act as, or from acting as, secretary or treasurer of a PCC.

     (2) If a person is convicted of an offence mentioned in Schedule 1 to the Children and Young Persons Act 1933, the person is disqualified –

     (a) from being nominated, chosen or elected as, or from serving as, a member of a PCC, a deanery synod, a diocesan synod or the General Synod;

(b) from being appointed to act as, or from acting as, secretary or treasurer of a PCC.

(3) If a person disqualified under paragraph (1) or (2) is a member of a PCC, a deanery synod, a diocesan synod or the House of Laity of the General Synod, the member's seat is vacated.

(4) A person's disqualification under paragraph (2) may be waived by the bishop of the diocese in question giving the person notice in writing; and the notice must specify the bishop's reasons for giving the waiver.

(5) Where a person whose seat has been vacated under paragraph (3) has his or her disqualification waived under paragraph (4), the person may resume his or her seat if it has remained vacant.

(6) A waiver under paragraph (4) –

(a) is of unlimited duration, and

(b) has effect in every diocese.

(7) Before deciding whether to give a waiver under paragraph (4), the bishop must consult –

(a) the diocesan safeguarding advisor, and

(b) such other persons as the bishop considers appropriate.

(8) On giving a notice under paragraph (4), the bishop must give a copy of the notice to the registrar of the diocese; and the registrar must file the copy in the diocesan registry.

Safeguarding cases: suspension

69 (1) This Rule applies where a member of a PCC or the secretary or treasurer of a PCC or a member of a deanery synod, a diocesan synod or the General Synod –

(a) is arrested on suspicion of committing an offence mentioned in Schedule 1 to the Children and Young Persons Act 1933, or

(b) is charged with an offence mentioned in that Schedule without being arrested.

(2) This Rule also applies where the bishop of a diocese is satisfied, on the basis of information provided by a local authority or the police, that a person of a description given in paragraph (1) presents a significant risk of harm.

(3) The bishop may suspend the person from the position in question by giving the person notice in writing; and the notice must specify the bishop's reasons for imposing the suspension.

(4) The bishop may at any time revoke the suspension by giving the person notice in writing.

(5)   For the purposes of paragraph (2), a person presents a significant risk of harm if there is a significant risk that the person may –

(a)   harm a child or vulnerable adult,

(b)   cause a child or vulnerable adult to be harmed,

(c)   put a child or vulnerable adult at risk of harm,

(d)   attempt to harm a child or vulnerable adult, or

(e)   incite another person to harm a child or vulnerable adult.

(6)   Before deciding whether to suspend a person under paragraph (3), or to revoke a suspension made under that paragraph, the bishop must consult –

(a)   the diocesan safeguarding advisor, and

(b)   such other persons as the bishop considers appropriate.

(7)   A suspension in a case within paragraph (1) continues (unless revoked under paragraph (4)) until the earlier of –

(a)   the expiry of three months beginning with the day on which the notice is given, and

(b)   the conclusion of the matter.

(8)   Where a person is suspended in a case within paragraph (1) and the matter is not concluded before the expiry of the three-month period referred to in paragraph (7)(a), a further notice of suspension may be given under paragraph (3); and paragraph (7) and this paragraph apply to the further suspension as they applied to the earlier suspension or suspensions.

(9)   A suspension in a case within paragraph (2) continues (unless revoked under paragraph (4)) until the expiry of three months beginning with the day on which the notice is given.

(10) Where a person is suspended in a case within paragraph (2), a further notice of suspension may be given under paragraph (3); and paragraph (9) and this paragraph apply to the further suspension as they applied to the earlier suspension or suspensions.

(11) Having given a notice of suspension or revocation under this Rule, the bishop must give each of the following written notification –

(a)   the clergy who hold office in the parish,

(b)   the churchwardens of the parish,

(c)   the registrar of the diocese,

(d)   the diocesan safeguarding advisor, and

(e)   such other persons as the bishop considers appropriate.

(12) The registrar must file a notification given under paragraph (11)(c) in the diocesan registry.

(13) For the purposes of this Rule, a matter is concluded when –

    (a) a decision is taken not to charge the person with the offence in question, or

    (b) where the person is charged with the offence, the proceedings for the offence are concluded.

Safeguarding cases: appeal against suspension

70 (1) A person who is given a notice of suspension under Rule 69(3) may appeal against the suspension in accordance with rules for the time being in force under section 83 of the Ecclesiastical Jurisdiction and Care of Churches Measure 2018.

(2) An appeal under this Rule must be made to the president of tribunals (as to whom, see section 4 of the Clergy Discipline Measure 2003).

(3) On an appeal under this Rule, the president of tribunals may, within 28 days following the lodging of the appeal, either confirm or revoke the suspension.

Safeguarding cases: interpretation

71 (1) In this Part of these Rules –

'barred list' has the same meaning as in the Safeguarding Vulnerable Groups Act 2006;

'child' means a person aged under 18;

'diocesan safeguarding advisor' means the person appointed as such under Canon C 30 for the diocese in question;

'vulnerable adult' has the same meaning as in the Safeguarding and Clergy Discipline Measure 2016.

(2) A reference in this Part of these Rules to an offence mentioned in Schedule 1 to the Children and Young Persons Act 1933 is a reference to an offence which is –

    (a) mentioned in that Schedule as amended, extended or applied from time to time, or

    (b) treated by an enactment (whenever passed or made) as if it were mentioned in that Schedule.

PART 8

MISCELLANEOUS

Personal data handling

72   A person who holds personal data about one or more other persons for the purposes of these Rules –

    (a)   must ensure that the personal data is held securely, and

    (b)   for that purpose, must have regard to such guidance as the Archbishops' Council may from time to time issue.

Casual vacancies

73   (1)   An election to fill a casual vacancy* under these Rules is to be conducted in the same manner as an ordinary election (unless the election takes place at a meeting held in accordance with Rule 45).

    (2)   The provisions of these Rules relating to casual vacancies –

        (a)   apply to the election of a member of a body constituted by or under these Rules;

        (b)   apply in relation to the choice of a person, with a reference to an election to fill a casual vacancy accordingly being read instead as a reference to a choice to fill one.

    (3)   A person elected or chosen to fill a casual vacancy holds office only for the unexpired portion of the term of office to be served in the case of that vacancy

Irregularities

74   (1)   Where irregularities are found during an election such that the presiding officer forms the opinion that the proceedings on the election should be declared null and void, the officer –

    (a)   must declare that the proceedings are null and void,

    (b)   must give notice to all electors of that declaration, and

    (c)   must cause a fresh election to be held.

---

*   'Casual vacancy' includes the case where there is a vacancy because not enough candidates were nominated to fill the places available: see rule 83(9).

(2) Where a notice is given under paragraph (1)(b), the election under paragraph (1)(c) must be completed within three months of the date of the notice.

(3) Where, in the case of an election to a diocesan synod, it is decided on an appeal that the election was not valid and the presiding officer is directed to hold a fresh election, the election must be completed within three months of the direction being given.

(4) Rule 45(3) (which provides for a casual vacancy in a diocesan synod to be filled within six months) accordingly does not apply if paragraph (3) of this Rule applies.

Constraints in elections

75 (1) Where there is a requirement in an election conducted under these Rules or under rules made under Rule 42 or 56 for a given number, or at least a given number, of the places available to be filled by candidates of a defined category, the presiding officer must examine the valid nominations to ascertain the number of candidates of that category.

(2) If the number of candidates of that category who are nominated is less than or equal to the required given number –

(a) those candidates are declared elected and their names are not included on the voting paper, and

(b) the requirement for a given number is disregarded and the election proceeds with the number of seats to be filled being reduced by the number of persons declared elected.

(3) The presiding officer must circulate with the voting papers a separate notice giving the name of each person who has been declared elected under paragraph (2).

(4) In the application of this Rule to an election which involves a system of electronic voting, a reference to something included on or circulated with a voting paper is to be read as including a reference to it being provided as part of the procedure provided for by the system being used in the election for electronic voting.

Communicating by email or post

76 (1) If a person has provided an email address –

(a) any communication required or authorised to be given to that person by or under these Rules may be sent to that email address, and

(b) any disclosure of the person's name and address required or authorised by or under these Rules must include that email address.

(2) A communication sent by email is to be treated as being in writing if it is received in a form which is legible and capable of being used for subsequent reference.

(3) Where a communication is sent to a person by email at the most recent address provided by that person, it is to be treated as having been given to the person at the time at which it is sent.

(4) Where a communication is sent to a person by post and addressed to that person at his or her last known address, it is to be treated as having been given to the person by the time at which it would be delivered in the ordinary course of post.

Implied power to vary or revoke

77 (1) A power conferred by these Rules to make, approve or pass a rule, order, resolution, determination, decision, appointment or scheme includes a power to vary or revoke it.

(2) A power conferred by these Rules to give a consent includes a power to vary or revoke the consent.

(3) A power conferred by these Rules to specify something includes a power to vary or revoke the specification.

(4) A power to vary or revoke is exercisable in the same manner and subject to the same conditions as the power to which it relates.

(5) This Rule does not apply to the power to give a waiver under Rule 68(4) (safeguarding: disqualification).

Power of bishop to make supplementary provision etc.

78 (1) In carrying out the provisions of these Rules in a diocese, the bishop of the diocese may exercise the following powers.

(2) The bishop may make provision for any matter not provided for in these Rules.

(3) The bishop may appoint a person to do something in respect of which there has been neglect or default by the person required by these Rules to do it.

(4) Where a PCC has no members or not enough members to be able to form the quorum for a meeting (see Rule M27), the bishop may appoint a person to do something which the PCC or an officer of the PCC is required to do by or under these Rules.

(5) The bishop may, so far as necessary for giving effect to the intention of a provision of these Rules –

(a) extend or alter the time for holding a meeting;

(b) modify the procedure for a meeting;

(c) extend or alter the time for holding an election;

(d) modify the procedure for an election.

(6) Paragraph (5)(c) and (d) does not apply to –

(a) an election to fill a casual vacancy,

(b) an election to the House of Laity of the General Synod, or

(c) an election to be held under Rule 74(1)(c) (fresh election following finding of irregularities).

(7) Where difficulties arise, the bishop may (subject to paragraphs (5) and (6)) give whatever directions he or she considers appropriate for removing those difficulties.

(8) This Rule does not authorise a bishop –

(a) to validate anything that was invalid when it was done, or

(b) to give a direction that is contrary to a resolution of the General Synod.

(9) In its application to the diocese in Europe, this Rule has effect as if the references to provisions of these Rules were references to such of those provisions as apply to that diocese.

Delegation by archbishop or bishop

79 (1) An archbishop or any other bishop of a diocese may appoint a commissary and delegate to that commissary some or all of the functions of the archbishop or other bishop under these Rules.

(2) But a bishop's functions as president of the diocesan synod may be delegated only to a person in episcopal orders.

(3) During a vacancy in an archbishopric, or where because of illness an archbishop is unable to exercise his or her functions as such under these Rules (including the power under paragraph (1)), the functions are exercisable by the other archbishop.

(4) During a vacancy in a diocesan bishopric, the functions of the bishop under these Rules (including those as president of the diocesan synod but not including the power under paragraph (1)) are exercisable by such person in episcopal orders as the archbishop of the province may appoint.

(5) Where because of illness, the bishop of a diocese is unable to exercise his or her functions as such under these Rules (including the power under paragraph (1)), the archbishop of the province may, if he or she thinks it necessary or appropriate, appoint a person in episcopal orders to exercise the functions.

(6)   If a person appointed under paragraph (1), (4) or (5) is a member of the house of clergy of a diocesan synod, that membership is suspended for the duration of the appointment.

(7)   If a person appointed under paragraph (4) or (5) becomes unable to act under the appointment because of illness, the archbishop may revoke the appointment and make a fresh one.

(8)   In its application to the diocese in Europe, this Rule has effect as if the references to these Rules were a reference to such of the provisions of these Rules as apply to that diocese.

(9)   The powers of an archbishop under this Rule in relation to the diocese in Europe are, subject to paragraph (3), exercisable by the Archbishop of Canterbury.

Validity of proceedings, etc.

80   (1)   The proceedings of a body constituted under these Rules are not invalidated by a vacancy in the membership of the body or a defect in the qualification, election, choice or appointment of any of its members.

(2)   Proceedings are not invalidated by the use of a form which differs from that specified by these Rules if the form used is to a substantially similar effect; and any question on that point is to be decided by the chancellor of the diocese.

(3)   Where there is an omission in a parish to prepare or maintain the roll or to hold the annual parochial church meeting, the rural dean must, on having the omission brought to his or her attention, ascertain the cause of the omission and report to the bishop of the diocese accordingly.

(4)   In its application to the diocese in Europe, this Rule has effect as if the references to these Rules were a reference to such of the provisions of these Rules as apply to that diocese.

Power of Business Committee to specify matters

81   (1)   A power conferred by these Rules on the Business Committee to specify something is exercisable by way of instrument.

(2)   An instrument under this Rule –

(a)   must be laid before the General Synod, and

(b)   does not come into force unless it has been approved by the Synod, with or without amendment.

(3)   If the Business Committee decides that an instrument under this Rule does not need to be debated by the Synod, it is to be treated as approved without

amendment for the purposes of paragraph (2) unless a member of the Synod gives notice under its Standing Orders that the member –

(a) wishes the matter to be debated, or

(b) wishes to move an amendment to it.

Interpretation: references to parishes and other areas

82 (1) In these Rules, 'parish' means –

(a) an ecclesiastical parish or a district constituted a 'conventional district' for the cure of souls;

(b) in relation to the diocese in Europe, a chaplaincy constituted as part of the diocese.

(2) A reference in these Rules to residence in a parish or deanery includes a reference to residence in any extra-parochial place which abuts the parish or deanery; and any question on that point is to be decided by the bishop's council and standing committee.

(3) A reference in these Rules to residence does not include a reference to residence of a casual nature.

(4) A reference in these Rules to the area of a benefice is, where –

(a) two or more benefices are held in plurality,

(b) there is, or is to be, a team ministry for the area of one of those benefices, and

(c) a pastoral scheme provides for extending the operation of the team ministry, so long as the plurality continues, to the area of any other benefice so held,

a reference to the combined area of the benefices concerned.

Interpretation: references to Church offices, structures etc.

83 (1) In these Rules, 'minister', in relation to a parish, means –

(a) the incumbent or priest in charge of the benefice to which the parish belongs or, in the case of a conventional district, the curate in charge, or

(b) a vicar in a team ministry to the extent that the duties of a minister are assigned to the vicar by a pastoral scheme or order or by the vicar's licence from the bishop.

(2) In these Rules, 'actual communicant' means a person –

(a) who has received Communion according to the use of the Church of England or a Church in communion with it at least three times during the 12 months preceding the date of the person becoming a member of a body the eligibility for membership of which depends on a person being an actual communicant, and

(b) who either is confirmed or ready and desirous of being confirmed or is receiving Communion as referred to in paragraph 1(b) of Canon B 15A (communicant members of other Churches subscribing to doctrine of Holy Trinity).

(3) A question as to whether a Church is in communion with the Church of England is to be decided for the purposes of these Rules by the Archbishop of Canterbury and the Archbishop of York acting jointly.

(4) Where a question as to whether a Church is in communion with the Church of England has been determined under section 6(2) of the Overseas and Other Clergy (Ministry and Ordination) Measure 1967, that determination has effect for the purposes of these Rules (as well as for the purposes of that Measure).

(5) In these Rules, 'public worship' means public worship according to the rites and ceremonies of the Church of England; and a reference in these Rules to a building licensed for public worship includes a reference to a building only part of which is so licensed.

(6) In these Rules, 'community roll', in relation to a cathedral church, means the roll kept in the case of that cathedral church for the purposes of section 9 of the Cathedrals Measure 1999 but for the purposes of these Rules, a person's name is to be treated as being on the community roll of a cathedral church only if the dean has declared the person to be a habitual worshipper.

(7) A reference in these Rules to a person's name being on the roll of a parish is, in the case of a person whose name is on the roll of a guild church, a reference to the person's name being on the roll of the parish in which the guild church is situated.

(8) In these Rules, 'guild church' means a church in the City of London designated and established as such under the City of London (Guild Churches) Acts 1952 and 1960.

(9) A reference in these Rules to the occurrence of a casual vacancy includes a reference to a case where there are not enough candidates nominated to fill the places available.

(10) A person who has executed a deed of relinquishment under the Clerical Disabilities Act 1870 is, for the purposes of these Rules, not to be treated as a clerk in Holy Orders (and is accordingly to be treated as a lay person) if –

(a) the deed has been enrolled in the High Court and recorded in the registry of a diocese under that Act, and

(b) no vacation of the enrolment of the deed is recorded in a diocesan registry under the Clerical Disabilities Act 1870 (Amendment) Measure 1934.

Interpretation: minor definitions

84 (1) In these Rules –

'Business Committee' means the Business Committee of the General Synod;

'the Constitution' means the Constitution of the General Synod as set out in Schedule 2 to this Measure;

'lay chair', in relation to a deanery synod, has the meaning given in Rule 26(7);

'mission initiative' has the meaning given in Part 7 of the Mission and Pastoral Measure 2011 (and, where a mission initiative has more than one leader, a reference to the leader is to be read as a reference to any of them);

'mission initiative roll' has the meaning given in Rule 27A;

'PCC' means parochial church council;

'personal data' has the same meaning as in the Data Protection Act 2018;

'register of clerical electors' and 'register of lay electors' each have the meaning given in Rule 27;

'the roll' has the meaning given in Rule 1(1).

(2) A reference in these Rules to something being in writing is to be read with Rule 76(2) (which makes provision about emails).

(3) A reference in these Rules to a numbered Form is a reference to the Form numbered as such in Part 10.

PART 9

PARISH GOVERNANCE: MODEL RULES

Section A: Annual Parochial Church Meeting

THE ANNUAL MEETING

Timing and attendance

M1 (1) In every parish, the annual parochial church meeting (referred to in this Part of these Rules as 'the annual meeting') must be held in the period which begins with 1 January and ends with 31 May.

(2) The following persons are entitled to attend the annual meeting and take part in its proceedings –

   (a) every lay person whose name is on the roll of the parish,

   (b) every clerk in Holy Orders to whom paragraph (3) applies,

   (c) where the parish is in the area of a benefice for which there is a team ministry, every member of the team,

   (d) where the parish is in the area of a group ministry, every incumbent and priest in charge in the group ministry, and

   (e) where the parish is in the area of a group ministry which includes the area of a benefice for which there is a team ministry, every vicar in the team ministry.

(3) This paragraph applies to a clerk in Holy Orders if he or she –

   (a) is beneficed in or licensed to the parish or to another parish in the area of the benefice to which the parish belongs,

   (b) is resident in the parish and is not beneficed in or licensed to any other parish,

   (c) does not come within sub-paragraph (a) or (b) but is declared by the PCC with the agreement of the minister to be a habitual worshipper in the parish, or

(d) is a co-opted member of the PCC under Rule M15(1)(k).

(4) A declaration under paragraph (3)(c) has effect until the earlier of –

(a) the conclusion of the annual meeting in the year in which a new roll is prepared under Rule 7, and

(b) the clerk in question ceasing to be a habitual worshipper in the parish.

Convening meeting

M2 (1) The minister* must convene the annual meeting by displaying a notice in Form M1 –

(a) in the case of the parish church or, where there is more than one church in the parish, each of those churches, on or near the principal door, and

(b) in the case of each building in the parish licensed for public worship, in a location readily visible to members of the congregation.

(2) The period for which a notice under paragraph (1) is on display must include the last two Sundays before the day of the meeting.

(3) The annual meeting must be held at a place in the parish unless the PCC decides otherwise.

(4) In a case where the minister is absent or incapacitated by illness or for some other reason or where there is nobody who is the minister within the meaning of these Rules (see Rule 83(1)), the minister's function under this Rule is to be carried out by –

(a) the vice-chair of the PCC, or

(b) if there is not a vice-chair or the vice-chair is unable or unwilling to act, the secretary of the PCC or some other person appointed by the PCC.

New parish: special meeting

M3 (1) Where the parish is a new parish created by a pastoral scheme, the minister of the new parish or, in the absence of a minister, a person appointed by the bishop of the diocese must, as soon as possible after the scheme comes into operation, convene a special parochial church meeting (referred to as 'the special meeting').

(2) The special meeting is to be treated for the purposes of these Rules as the annual meeting for the year in which it is held.

(3) Subject to that, the provisions of these Rules relating to the convening or conduct of the annual meeting apply to the special meeting.

---

*   See Rule 83(1) for the definition of 'minister'.

PROCEEDINGS AND ELECTIONS

Chair

M4 (1) The chair of the annual meeting is –

    (a) the minister, or

    (b) if the minister is absent or decides to vacate the chair or if there is nobody who is the minister within the meaning of these Rules (see Rule 83(1)), the vice-chair of the PCC, or

    (c) if the vice-chair of the PCC is absent or decides not to take the chair –

        (i) a person chosen by the annual meeting, or

        (ii) if the parish belongs to a benefice for which there is a team ministry and paragraph (2) applies, the rector in the team ministry.

(2) This paragraph applies if –

    (a) a vicar in the team ministry has the function of chairing the annual meeting (or a share in discharging that function) by virtue of a pastoral scheme or bishop's licence, and

    (b) the vicar is absent but the rector in the team ministry is present.

(3) If there is an equality of votes, the chair of the meeting has a second, casting vote, except in the case of an election taking place at the annual meeting (as to which, see Rule M9(8)).

Business: reports etc.

M5 (1) The PCC must provide the annual meeting with each of the following, which the annual meeting may then discuss –

    (a) a report on the changes to the roll since the last annual meeting or, in a year in which a new roll is prepared, a report on the numbers entered on the new roll,

    (b) an annual report on the proceedings of the PCC and the activities of the parish generally,

    (c) the financial statements of the PCC for the year ending on the 31 December preceding the meeting,

    (d) the annual fabric report under section 50 of the Ecclesiastical Jurisdiction and Care of Churches Measure 2018, and

    (e) a report of the proceedings of the deanery synod.

(2) The PCC must ensure that a copy of the roll is available for inspection at the meeting.

(3) The annual report to be provided under paragraph (1)(b) must include a statement as to whether the PCC has complied with the duty under section 5 of the Safeguarding and Clergy Discipline Measure 2016 (duty to have regard to House of Bishops' guidance on safeguarding children and vulnerable adults).

(4) The annual report to be provided under paragraph (1)(b) must be prepared in the form specified by the Business Committee.

(5) The financial statements to be provided under paragraph (1)(c) –

(a) must be prepared in the form specified by the Business Committee, and

(b) must be independently examined or audited in the manner specified by the Business Committee.

(6) If the PCC approves the financial statements that have been examined or audited under paragraph (5)(b), the chair of the meeting at which they are approved must sign them.

(7) Once the financial statements have been signed under paragraph (6), the PCC must, for at least seven days before the annual meeting –

(a) publish the signed statements in such form (whether electronic or otherwise) as it decides, and

(b) make a copy of the signed statements available for inspection, on a reasonable request being made.

(8) The PCC must, before the end of 28 days beginning with the date of the annual meeting, ensure that a copy of the annual report and financial statements provided under paragraph (1)(b) and (c) are given to the secretary of the diocesan board of finance for it to retain.

Business: elections and appointments

M6 (1) The annual meeting must, in the manner provided by Rule M9, do the following things in the following order –

(a) elect in every third year* parochial representatives of the laity to the deanery synod;

(b) elect parochial representatives of the laity to the PCC.

(2) The annual meeting, having conducted the elections under paragraph (1), must appoint a person who is not a member of the PCC to be the independent examiner or auditor of the PCC for a term of office ending at the conclusion of the next annual meeting.

---

* The next elections are to be held in 2023.

(3) It is for the PCC to pay the remuneration of a person appointed under paragraph (2).

(4) A person may be appointed as the independent examiner of the PCC only if the person comes within the description given in section 145(1)(a) of the Charities Act 2011 (independent person with requisite ability and experience etc.).

(5) A person may be appointed as the auditor of the PCC only if the person is eligible as the auditor of a charity under section 144(2) of that Act (eligibility as statutory auditor).

(6) The annual meeting may not appoint sidesmen; the duty to do so is imposed on the PCC by section 2(2)(f) of the Parochial Church Councils (Powers) Measure 1956.

(7) In the case of a new parish (see Rule M3), a special meeting must (in addition to its other business) decide on the number of members of the PCC who are to be elected representatives of the laity until the annual meeting held in the following year; and that number need not accord with the number provided for under Rule M15(8).

Business: miscellaneous

M7 (1) Any person who is entitled to attend the annual meeting may ask a question about parochial church matters or bring about a discussion of any matter of parochial or general church interest –

    (a) by moving a general resolution, or

    (b) by moving to make a particular recommendation to the council in relation to its duties.

(2) The annual meeting –

    (a) may adjourn;

    (b) may determine its own rules of procedure.

(3) The secretary of the PCC, or such other person as the meeting may appoint instead, acts as the clerk of the annual meeting and must record the minutes.

Qualifications of persons to be elected

M8 (1) A person is qualified for election as a parochial representative of the laity to the deanery synod or PCC under Rule M6(1)(a) or (b) if –

    (a) the person is aged 16 or over,

    (b) he or she is an actual communicant, and

      (c)   his or her name is on the roll of the parish and, unless he or she is aged under 18 at the date of the election, has been on the roll for at least the preceding six months.

(2)   But if the person has his or her name on the roll of more than one parish, he or she must choose one of the parishes concerned for the purpose of qualifying for election as a parochial representative of the laity to the deanery synod.

(3)   A person may not be nominated for election under Rule M6(1)(a) or (b) unless –

      (a)   the person has indicated his or her consent to serve, or

      (b)   there is, in the opinion of the meeting, sufficient evidence of his or her willingness to serve.

(4)   A person may not be nominated for election under Rule M6(1)(a) if the person is disqualified under Part 7.

(5)   The annual meeting may by resolution decide that a person who serves as a parochial representative of the laity on the deanery synod for the whole or any part of each of a specified number of successive terms of office may not be nominated for election under Rule M6(1)(a) to serve as such for the whole or any part of the term of office immediately following the last of those terms.

(6)   A resolution under paragraph (5) may not apply to a term of office –

      (a)   which began before 1 January 2020 (being the commencement date of the Church Representation and Ministers Measure 2019 which substituted the whole of the Church Representation Rules), or

      (b)   which the person concerned is serving as a result of having been elected to fill a casual vacancy.*

(7)   A resolution under paragraph (5) may be amended or revoked by a subsequent annual meeting or special parochial church meeting.

(8)   A person may not be nominated for election under Rule M6(1)(b) if –

      (a)   the person is disqualified under Part 7, or

      (b)   the person is disqualified from being the trustee of a charity (and the disqualification is not subject to a waiver which permits membership of a PCC).

Conduct of an election

M9 (1)   This Rule applies in the case of every election which is to take place at the annual meeting, subject to any variations made by a resolution under Rule M10 or M11.

---

*   'Casual vacancy' includes the case where there is a vacancy because not enough candidates were nominated to fill the places available: see Rule 83(9).

(2) A candidate must be nominated, either before the meeting in writing or at the meeting, by two persons each of whom –

    (a) must be entitled to attend the meeting, and

    (b) must have his or her name on the roll of a parish.

(3) If the number of candidates does not exceed the number of seats to be filled, each candidate is declared elected.

(4) If the number of candidates exceeds the number of seats to be filled, an election must take place in accordance with the following provisions.

(5) Every lay person whose name is on the roll of the parish is entitled to vote in the election.

(6) Each person entitled to vote has as many votes as there are seats to be filled, but may not give more than one vote to the same candidate.

(7) Votes may be given by a show of hands; but if one or more persons object to that, each vote is to be given on a voting paper signed on the back by the voter.

(8) If there is an equality of votes, the election is decided by the drawing of a lot by the presiding officer.

(9) On a recount of an election or a stage of an election, either on an appeal or at the request of the presiding officer or a candidate, if the original count and the recount are identical at the point when a lot must be drawn, the original lot must be used to decide.

(10) The presiding officer for an election at the annual meeting is the chair of the meeting, unless a presiding officer is appointed under Rule M11(3).

Adoption of STV system

M10 (1) The annual meeting may resolve that the election of parochial representatives of the laity (whether to the deanery synod or to the PCC or to both) is to be conducted by the single transferable vote system.

(2) A resolution under this Rule is valid only if it is approved by at least two-thirds of those present and voting at the meeting; and it does not take effect until the next annual meeting.

(3) Where a resolution under this Rule is passed, the election is to be held in accordance with the rules for the time being in force under the General Synod's Standing Orders; and those rules have effect for that purpose with whatever modifications are necessary.

Postal voting

M11(1)   The annual meeting may resolve that a person entitled to attend the meeting and vote in the election of parochial representatives of the laity may apply on Form M2 for a postal vote.

(2)   A resolution under this Rule is valid only if it is approved by at least two-thirds of those present and voting at the meeting; and it does not take effect until the next annual meeting.

(3)   Where applications for a postal vote have been received by the date specified in the notice convening the next annual meeting and the number of candidates nominated exceeds the number of seats to be filled, that annual meeting must appoint a presiding officer; and the person appointed may not be a candidate in the election.

(4)   At that annual meeting, a voting paper must be given to each person present who is entitled to vote; and completed voting papers must be returned into the custody of the presiding officer before the close of the meeting.

(5)   The presiding officer must ensure that each person who has applied for a postal vote on Form M2 is given a voting paper within seven days of the close of the meeting.

(6)   A vote is counted only if it is given on a voting paper –

(a)   which is marked in the manner indicated on the paper,

(b)   the back of which is signed by the elector, and

(c)   which is returned to the presiding officer within 14 days of the close of the meeting.

Result of an election

M12(1)   The result of an election held at the annual meeting, or which involved postal voting in accordance with a resolution under Rule M11, must be announced as soon as practicable by the presiding officer.

(2)   A notice of the result must be displayed –

(a)   in the case of the parish church or, where there is more than one church in the parish, each of those churches, on or near the principal door, and

(b)   in the case of each building in the parish licensed for public worship, in a location readily visible to members of the congregation.

(3)   A notice under paragraph (2) must remain on display for at least 14 days.

(4)   The notice must specify the date on which the result was declared.

(5)   After the end of the period for which the notice was on display under paragraph (3), the secretary of the PCC must keep a list of every member's name and address.

(6)   The list under paragraph (5) must be made available for inspection, on reasonable notice being given to the secretary by a person who is resident in the parish or has his or her name on the roll; but the secretary need not provide a copy of the list.

(7)   Where a member has provided the secretary with an email address, the address recorded for that member on the list must include that email address.

(8)   The list in the form in which it is made available under paragraph (6) must include every name recorded on it but no other personal data.

(9)   The secretary of the PCC must give the name and address of every person elected to the deanery synod as a parochial representative of the laity to –

(a)   the diocesan electoral registration officer, and

(b)   the secretary of the deanery synod.

SPECIAL AND EXTRAORDINARY MEETINGS

Special meeting

M13(1)   The minister may convene a special parochial church meeting in addition to the annual meeting; and the minister must do so if at least one-third of the lay members of the PCC make a written representation to him or her for there to be such a meeting.

(2)   The provisions of these Rules relating to the convening or conduct of the annual meeting apply, with whatever modifications are necessary, to a special parochial church meeting.

(3)   The following persons are entitled to attend a special parochial church meeting –

(a)   every lay person whose name is on the roll of the parish on the day which is 21 clear days before the day on which the meeting is to be held, and

(b)   every clerk in Holy Orders who would be entitled to attend the annual meeting if it were to be held on the day on which the special meeting is to be held.

(4)   In a case where the minister is absent or incapacitated by illness or for some other reason or where there is nobody who is the minister within the meaning

of these Rules (see Rule 83(1)), the minister's function under this Rule is to be carried out by –

(a) the vice-chair of the PCC, or

(b) if there is not a vice-chair or the vice-chair is unable or unwilling to act, the secretary of the PCC or some other person appointed by the PCC.

Extraordinary meeting

M14(1) The archdeacon whose archdeaconry includes the parish must, subject to paragraphs (2) and (3), convene an extraordinary parochial church meeting if –

(a) at least one-third of the lay members of the PCC or one-tenth of the persons whose names are on the roll of the parish make a written representation to the archdeacon to that effect, and

(b) the archdeacon considers that the representation is made with sufficient cause.

(2) Where the archdeacon is the minister, the bishop of the diocese or a person appointed by the bishop must, subject to paragraph (3), convene an extraordinary parochial church meeting if –

(a) at least one-third of the lay members of the PCC or one-tenth of the persons whose names are on the roll of the parish make a representation to the bishop for there to be such a meeting, and

(b) the bishop or a person appointed by the bishop considers that the representation is made with sufficient cause.

(3) The duty under paragraph (1) or (2) does not arise if, in response to the representation, an extraordinary meeting of the PCC is convened under Rule M33.

(4) At a meeting convened under this Rule, the person who convened the meeting must either take the chair or appoint someone else to do so.

(5) If the chair of the meeting would not otherwise be entitled to attend, he or she may not vote on any resolution before the meeting.

(6) The following persons are entitled to attend an extraordinary parochial church meeting –

(a) every lay person whose name is on the roll of the parish on the day which is 21 clear days before the day on which the meeting is to be held, and

(b) every clerk in Holy Orders who would be entitled to attend the annual meeting if it were to be held on the day on which the extraordinary meeting is to be held.

Section B: Parochial Church Council

MEMBERSHIP

Members

M15(1) The members of the PCC are –

(a) every clerk in Holy Orders who is beneficed in or licensed to the parish,

(b) any clerk in Holy Orders who is authorised to chair meetings of the PCC under Rule M26,

(c) any deaconess or lay worker licensed to the parish,

(d) if the parish is in the area of a benefice for which there is a team ministry, every member of the team,

(e) the churchwardens of the parish,

(f) any person chosen as a churchwarden of the parish but not yet admitted to office as such,

(g) any deputy churchwarden who is an ex officio member under a scheme under Rule M34 or M35,

(h) if the annual meeting decides that one or more of the readers licensed to the parish or to an area including the parish whose names are on the roll of the parish should be members, the reader or readers in question,

(i) every person whose name is on the roll of the parish and who is a lay member of a deanery synod, a diocesan synod or the General Synod,

(j) the elected representatives of the laity, with the number being determined under paragraphs (8) and (9), and

(k) any clerk in Holy Orders, or any actual communicant aged 16 or over, whom the PCC decides to co-opt as a member, with the number being determined under paragraph (10).

(2) A clerk in Holy Orders (other than the minister) is not eligible for membership under paragraph (1)(a) or (d) if, were he or she to become a member, the number of clerical members would equal or exceed the number of lay members.

(3) Where there are two or more clerks in Holy Orders who (but for this paragraph) would become eligible under paragraph (1)(a) or (d) on the same day, paragraph (2) applies to each of those clerks taken together; and, accordingly, in a case within paragraph (2), none of them are eligible for membership under paragraph (1)(a) or (d) (as the case may be).

(4) A person is eligible for membership under paragraph (1)(e), (f) or (g) only if the person is an actual communicant whose name is on the roll of the parish.

(5) For the purposes of paragraph (1)(i), a lay member of a deanery synod who is a parochial representative elected by the annual meeting of the parish is eligible only for membership of the PCC for the parish, even if the person's name is on the roll of one or more other parishes.

(6) For the purposes of paragraph (1)(i), a lay member of a deanery synod who is a member of the synod otherwise than by virtue of election as a parochial representative and whose name is on the roll of the parish and on the roll of one or more other parishes –

(a) must choose one of the parishes concerned, and

(b) is accordingly eligible only for membership of the PCC for the parish if it is the parish which he or she chooses.

(7) For the purposes of paragraph (1)(i), a lay member of a diocesan synod or a member of the House of Laity of the General Synod whose name is on the roll of the parish and on the roll of one or more other parishes –

(a) must choose one of the parishes concerned, and

(b) is accordingly eligible only for membership of the PCC for the parish if it is the parish which he or she chooses.

(8) The number of representatives of the laity for the purposes of paragraph (1)(j) is –

(a) if there are no more than 50 names on the roll, six;

(b) if there are more than 50 but no more than 100, nine;

(c) if there are more than 100, a further three per hundred names and, where the number of names on the roll is not divisible by 100 without fraction or remainder, for the fraction or remainder, up to a maximum of 15.

(9) The annual meeting may by resolution vary the number of representatives there would otherwise be for the parish under paragraph (8); but a resolution under this paragraph does not take effect before the next annual meeting.

(10) The number of members under paragraph (1)(k) is either two or any greater number which does not exceed one-fifth of the number of members under paragraph (1)(j).

(11) A person whose name is removed from the roll of the parish on a revision under Rule 4 ceases to be a member of the PCC on the date on which the revised roll is completed.

(12) A person who does not make a fresh application for enrolment when a new roll of the parish is being prepared ceases to be a member of the PCC on the date on which the new roll is completed.

(13) A person who is or becomes disqualified as a member of the PCC (whether under Part 7 or otherwise) ceases to be a member on the date on which the disqualification takes effect.

(14) In a case within paragraph (11) or (12), the PCC may nonetheless co-opt the person concerned as a member under paragraph (1)(k).

Term of office: representatives of the laity

M16(1) A person who is a member of the PCC under Rule M15(1)(j) (representatives of laity) holds office as such for a period which –

    (a) begins with the conclusion of the annual meeting at which the person was elected as a representative of the laity, and

    (b) ends with the conclusion of the third subsequent annual meeting.

(2) But the annual meeting may, despite paragraph (1)(b), decide that the members under Rule M15(1)(j) are to retire at the conclusion of the annual meeting following their election.

(3) A decision under paragraph (2) does not affect the term of office of a member due to retire from the PCC at the conclusion of the annual meeting held after the one at which the decision was taken.

(4) A decision under paragraph (2) must be reviewed by the annual meeting at least once every six years; and if, on the review, the annual meeting revokes the decision, paragraph (1) applies unless and until a further decision is taken under paragraph (2).

(5) Where a decision is not taken under paragraph (2), one-third of the members under Rule M15(1)(j) are to retire and be elected each year; but at an annual meeting at which more than one-third of the members under Rule M15(1)(j) are elected, lots are drawn to decide which third is to retire in the first year after that meeting, which third in the second year and which third in the third year.

(6) A member under Rule M15(1)(j) is, subject to paragraphs (7) and (8), eligible on retirement for re-election.

(7) The annual meeting may decide that nobody who is a member under Rule M15(1)(j) may hold office as such after the date of the meeting for a continuous period which exceeds whatever number of years the annual meeting decides.

(8) The annual meeting may also decide that a person who, as a result of a decision under paragraph (7), has ceased to be eligible to be a member under Rule M15(1(j) may, after such interval as the annual meeting decides, again stand for election as a representative of the laity.

(9)   Where a member under Rule M15(1)(j) resigns or otherwise fails to serve the full term of office, the casual vacancy is to be filled for the remainder of the term in accordance with Rule M18.

(10) A reference in this Rule to the conclusion of an annual meeting is, in a case where an election held at the meeting also involves postal voting, to be read as a reference to the declaration of the result of the election.

Term of office: other cases

M17(1)   A person who is a member of the PCC under Rule M15(1)(f) (churchwarden elect) holds office as such for the period which –

(a)   begins when the person is chosen as churchwarden, and

(b)   ends when the person is admitted to the office of churchwarden (at which point the person continues as a member, holding office as such under Rule M15(1)(e)).

(2)   A person who is a member of the PCC under Rule M15(1)(h) (readers) holds office as such for the period which –

(a)   begins with the conclusion of the annual meeting at which it was decided that the person should be a member, and

(b)   ends with the conclusion of the next annual meeting, unless it is decided at that meeting that the person should continue to be a member.

(3)   A person who is a member of the PCC under Rule M15(1)(i) as an elected lay member of a deanery synod holds office as a member of the PCC for the period which –

(a)   begins with the date of election, and

(b)   ends with the next 30 June following the annual meeting at which elections of parochial representatives of the laity to the deanery synod are required to be held under Rule M6(1)(a).

(4)   A person who is a member of the PCC under Rule M15(1)(k) (co-opted members) holds office as such for the period which –

(a)   begins when the decision to co-opt the person as a member takes effect, and

(b)   ends with the conclusion of the next annual meeting.

(5)   Paragraph (4)(b) does not prevent the person being co-opted on subsequent occasions for a similar term.

Casual vacancies

M18(1)   A casual vacancy* among the parochial representatives elected to a PCC must be filled as soon as practicable after the vacancy occurs.

(2)   Where the annual meeting is not due to be held within the two months following the occurrence of the vacancy, the vacancy may be filled by the election by the PCC of a person qualified to be elected as a parochial representative.

OFFICERS

Chair and vice-chair

M19(1)   The minister is the chair of the PCC.

(2)   The PCC must elect a lay member as vice-chair; and the vice-chair acts as chair and accordingly has the powers vested in the chair –

(a)   where there is no minister,

(b)   where the minister is absent or unable to act for some other reason, or

(c)   where the minister invites the vice-chair to act as chair.

(3)   Where a special cure of souls in respect of the parish has been assigned to a vicar in a team ministry or a special responsibility for pastoral care in respect of the parish has been assigned to a member of the team under section 34(8) of the Mission and Pastoral Measure 2011 –

(a)   the vicar or team member in question is to be treated as the minister for the purposes of this Rule, or

(b)   if the vicar or team member is absent or incapacitated by illness or for some other reason, the rector in the team ministry is to be treated as the minister for those purposes.

Secretary and treasurer

M20(1)   The PCC may appoint one of its members as secretary; but if it does not, it must appoint some other fit person.

(2)   The secretary has the following functions –

---

*   'Casual vacancy' includes the case where there is a vacancy because not enough candidates were nominated to fill the places available: see rule 83(9).

    (a)   to have charge of all the documents relating to the current business of the PCC other than the roll of the parish (unless the secretary is also the electoral roll officer);

    (b)   to keep the minutes;

    (c)   to record all resolutions passed;

    (d)   to notify his or her name and address to the secretary of the deanery synod and the secretary of the diocesan synod.

(3)   The PCC may appoint one of its members as treasurer or two or more of its members as joint treasurers; but if it does not, it must –

    (a)   arrange for the office of treasurer to be discharged by such of the churchwardens as are members of the PCC or, if only one of them is a member, by that one solely, or

    (b)   appoint some other fit person.

(4)   Where the person appointed as secretary or treasurer is not a member of the PCC, he or she does not become a member merely as a result of holding the office in question but may be co-opted under Rule M15(1)(k).

Electoral roll officer

M21(1)   The PCC must appoint a person as electoral roll officer to act under its direction for the purpose of carrying out its functions with regard to the roll of the parish.

(2)   The electoral roll officer accordingly has charge of the roll of the parish and must keep it up to date in accordance with these Rules.

(3)   The person appointed under paragraph (1) need not be a member of the PCC and may also be the secretary.

Independent examiner or auditor

M22(1)   If the annual meeting does not appoint an independent examiner or auditor to the PCC, or the person appointed is unable or unwilling to act, the PCC must appoint some other fit person.

(2)   A person appointed under paragraph (1) must not be a member of the PCC.

(3)   Paragraphs (4) and (5) of Rule M6 (eligibility for appointment as independent examiner or auditor) apply to an appointment under paragraph (1) of this Rule as they apply to an appointment under paragraph (2) of that Rule.

(4)   The term of office of a person appointed under paragraph (1) ends at the conclusion of the next annual meeting.

(5)   It is for the PCC to pay the remuneration of a person appointed under paragraph (1).

BUSINESS

Meetings: time and place

M23(1)   Each year, the PCC must hold a sufficient number of meetings to enable the efficient transaction of its business.

(2)   The chair must convene each of those meetings.

(3)   The chair may at any other time convene a meeting of the PCC; but if the chair does not do so within seven days of receiving a demand for such a meeting signed by at least one-third of the members of the PCC, those members may themselves immediately convene a meeting.

(4)   A meeting of the PCC is to be held at such place as the PCC directs or, in the absence of such a direction, as the chair directs.

Meetings: attendance

M24(1)   A person is entitled to attend a meeting of the PCC only if –

(a)   the person is a member of the PCC, or

(b)   where the parish is in the area of a group ministry, the person is entitled to do so under paragraph (2).

(2)   Where the parish is in the area of a group ministry, each of the following persons is entitled to attend a meeting of the PCC –

(a)   every incumbent of a benefice in the group,

(b)   every priest in charge of a benefice in the group, and

(c)   if the area of the group ministry includes the area of a benefice for which there is a team ministry, every vicar in the team ministry.

(3)   A person who is entitled under paragraph (2) to attend a meeting of the PCC –

(a)   is entitled to receive documents circulated to the members of the PCC, and

(b)   is entitled to speak at the meeting, but

(c)   is not entitled to vote at the meeting.

(4)   The PCC may invite such other persons to attend its meetings as it wishes.

Meetings: notice

M25 (1) At least ten clear days before a meeting of the PCC (other than one convened under paragraph (8)), notice of the meeting must be displayed –

  (a) in the case of the parish church or, where there is more than one church in the parish, each of those churches, on or near the principal door, and

  (b) in the case of each building in the parish licensed for public worship, in a location readily visible to members of the congregation.

(2) A notice under paragraph (1) must –

  (a) specify the time and place of the meeting, and

  (b) be signed by or on behalf of the chair or other persons convening the meeting.

(3) At least seven clear days before a meeting of the PCC (other than one convened under paragraph (8)), notice of the meeting must be given to –

  (a) each member of the PCC,

  (b) where the parish is in the area of a group ministry, each person entitled to attend the meeting under Rule M24(2), and

  (c) each person whom the PCC has invited to the meeting under Rule M24(4).

(4) A notice under paragraph (3) must –

  (a) specify the time and place of the meeting,

  (b) be signed by or on behalf of the secretary, and

  (c) contain the agenda of the meeting, including any motions or other business proposed by members of which the secretary has received notice.

(5) But in the case of a meeting of the PCC which immediately follows the annual meeting and which has been called only for the purpose of appointing or electing officers of the PCC or the members of the standing committee, notice is not required under paragraph (3) if it has been given under paragraph (1).

(6) If the chair, vice-chair and secretary, or any two of them, consider for some good and sufficient reason that a meeting of the PCC which has been convened should be postponed, each member of the PCC and each person specified in Rule M24(2) must be given –

  (a) notice that the meeting has been postponed, and

  (b) notice specifying the time and place of the reconvened meeting.

(7) A notice under paragraph (6)(b) must be given before the end of 14 days beginning with the date for which the meeting had been convened.

(8)   In the event of a sudden emergency or other special circumstances requiring immediate action by the PCC, the chair may convene a meeting by giving every member whatever written notice is practicable.

Meetings: chair

M26(1)   The chair at a meeting of the PCC (other than an extraordinary meeting under Rule M33) is –

    (a)   the chair of the PCC, or

    (b)   if the chair is not present, the vice-chair of the PCC, or

    (c)   if nobody is available under sub-paragraph (a) or (b) (whether to chair the whole meeting or particular items on the agenda), a person chosen by and from the members of the PCC.

(2)   Where a clerk in Holy Orders who is licensed to officiate in the parish or has permission to do so is authorised by the bishop to act as the chair of the PCC –

    (a)   that clerk is to be the chair of the PCC for the meeting if the chair of the PCC is absent, and

    (b)   the references in paragraph (1) to the chair are accordingly to be read as references to that clerk.

(3)   An authorisation of the kind mentioned in paragraph (2) may be given only if –

    (a)   the clerk in question agrees, and

    (b)   an application is made by the minister and PCC jointly or, where the benefice is vacant, by the PCC alone.

(4)   The chair at a meeting of the PCC must vacate the chair, either generally or for the purposes of any business in which he or she has a personal interest or any other particular business, if –

    (a)   the chair thinks it appropriate to do so, or

    (b)   the meeting so resolves with the agreement of the archdeacon.

Meetings: procedure

M27(1)   The quorum for a meeting of the PCC is (subject to paragraph (2)) –

    (a)   one-third of its members, or

    (b)   in the case of a meeting convened under Rule M25(8) (emergency etc.), a majority of its members.

(2)   A meeting of the PCC is quorate only if the majority of the members present are lay persons.

(3) Business which is not specified in the agenda for a meeting of the PCC may not be transacted at the meeting except with the consent of at least three-quarters of the members present; and at a meeting convened under Rule M25(8), the only business which may be transacted is that specified in the notice convening the meeting.

(4) Business at a meeting of the PCC is decided by a majority of the members present and voting.

(5) In the case of an equality of votes at a meeting of the PCC, the chair has a second, casting vote.

(6) A meeting of the PCC may adjourn its proceedings to such time and place as the meeting may decide.

Meetings: minutes

M28(1) The minutes of each meeting of the PCC must record the name of each member present at the meeting and any other person attending.

(2) If one-fifth of the members of the PCC present and voting on a resolution so require, the minutes must record the name of each member voting for the resolution and the name of each member voting against.

(3) A member of the PCC may require the minutes to record how he or she voted on a particular resolution.

(4) Each member of the PCC, and any person entitled to attend meetings of the PCC under Rule M24(2), is entitled to have access to the minutes of the meetings of the PCC.

(5) Each of the following persons is entitled to have access to the approved minutes of meetings of the PCC without the authority of the PCC –

(a) the independent examiner or auditor of the PCC's financial statements,

(b) the bishop,

(c) the archdeacon, and

(d) any person authorised in writing by a person mentioned in sub-paragraph (a), (b) or (c).

(6) Any other person whose name is on the roll of the parish is entitled to have access to the approved minutes of meetings of the PCC held after the annual meeting in 1995, except any minutes which the PCC regards as confidential.

(7) Other persons may have access to the minutes of the meetings of the PCC only in accordance with a specific authorisation from the PCC; but, where minutes have been deposited in the diocesan record office under the Parochial Registers and Records Measure 1978, the need for that authorisation may be dispensed with by the chief officer of that office.

Business by correspondence

M29(1)   The chair of the PCC may, if he or she considers that any business can properly be conducted by correspondence, instruct the secretary of the PCC to send proposals requiring the approval of members to –

(a)   each member of the PCC, and

(b)   any person entitled to attend the meetings of the PCC under Rule M24(2).

(2)   Unless objection to the proposals is received from members in such numbers and within such period from the date of their being sent as the chair of the PCC may specify, the proposals are to be treated at the end of that period as approved by the PCC as if they had been approved at a duly convened meeting.

(3)   Where proposals are circulated under this Rule for approval, the secretary must report to the next meeting of the PCC –

(a)   whether the proposals were approved, and

(b)   if objections to the proposals were received, the number of members from whom they were received.

Audit of financial statements

M30(1)   The independent examiner or auditor of the PCC's financial statements –

(a)   is entitled to have access to books, documents or other records (however kept) which relate to the financial statements;

(b)   may require information and explanations from past or present treasurers or members of the PCC.

(2)   If a person fails to comply with a requirement under paragraph (1)(b), the independent examiner or auditor may apply to the Charity Commission for an order for directions under section 155 of the Charities Act 2011.

Standing committee

M31(1)   The PCC has a standing committee constituted in accordance with this Rule.

(2)   If there are more than 50 names on the roll of the parish on the date on which the annual meeting is held, the standing committee is to consist of –

(a)   the minister,

(b)   each churchwarden who is a member of the PCC or, if there are more than two, such two or more of them as are appointed by the PCC by resolution, and

> (c) at least two other members of the PCC appointed by the PCC by resolution, the number of whom must be at least equal to the number of churchwardens who are members of the committee under sub-paragraph (b).

(3) If there are no more than 50 names on the roll of the parish on the date on which the annual meeting is held, the standing committee is to consist of –

> (a) the minister, and
>
> (b) at least two other members of the PCC (each of whom may, but need not, be a churchwarden) appointed by the PCC by resolution.

(4) The PCC may by resolution remove a person appointed under paragraph (2)(b) or (c) or (3)(b).

(5) A member appointed under paragraph (2)(b) or (c) or (3)(b) holds office for a period which begins with the date of appointment and ends with the conclusion of the next annual meeting (subject to the possibility of the member's removal under paragraph (4)).

(6) The standing committee may transact the PCC's business between meetings of the PCC; but the standing committee –

> (a) may not discharge a duty of the PCC, and
>
> (b) may not exercise a power of the PCC which is subject to the passing of a resolution by the PCC or compliance by the PCC with some other requirement.

(7) If the PCC gives the standing committee any directions as to the exercise of its power under paragraph (6), the committee must exercise the power in accordance with those directions.

Other committees

M32 (1) The PCC may appoint committees for the various branches of church work in the parish; and the members of a committee appointed under this Rule may include persons who are not members of the PCC.

(2) The minister is entitled to be an ex officio member of each committee appointed under this Rule.

Extraordinary meetings

M33 (1) Where a written representation is made for the purposes of Rule M14, the archdeacon or bishop must, if he or she does not convene an extraordinary parochial church meeting under that Rule, convene an extraordinary meeting of the PCC under this Rule.

(2) At a meeting convened under this Rule, the archdeacon or bishop must either take the chair or appoint a person to do so.

(3) If the chair of the meeting would not otherwise be entitled to attend, he or she may not vote on any resolution before it.

SCHEMES

Parish with more than one place of worship: election of representatives of laity

M34 (1) If there are in the parish two or more churches* or buildings licensed for public worship, the annual meeting may make a scheme for the election of representatives of the laity to the PCC in a way that is intended to make due provision for the representation of the congregation of each church or building.

(2) A scheme under this Rule may provide for –

(a) the election or choice of one or two deputy churchwardens,

(b) the delegation by the churchwardens to the deputy or deputies of such functions relating to a church or building licensed for public worship as are specified in the scheme, and

(c) the deputy or each of the deputies to be an ex officio member of the PCC.

(3) A scheme under this Rule may include provision under Rule M35.

(4) A scheme under this Rule comes into operation on the day specified in the scheme.

(5) Where a scheme is made under this Rule, a copy of the scheme –

(a) must be filed in the diocesan registry, and

(b) must be sent to the secretary of the bishop's council and standing committee.

(6) This Rule does not affect the appointment, in parishes with more than one parish church, of two churchwardens for each church under section 1(2)(a) of the Churchwardens Measure 2001.

---

* 'Church' means any church or chapel which has been consecrated for the purpose of public worship according to the rites and ceremonies of the Church of England: see section 3, Interpretation Measure 1925.

Parish with more than one place of worship: district church council

M35 (1) If there are in the parish two or more churches* or buildings licensed for public worship, the annual meeting may make a scheme for –

  (a) the establishment of a body called a 'district church council', the purpose of which is to carry out in relation to a specified district in the parish in which there is at least one church or building licensed for public worship such functions of the PCC as are delegated to it, and

  (b) the election by the annual meeting of the district of representatives of the laity to the district church council.

(2) A scheme under this Rule must include provision for –

  (a) ex officio membership of the district church council, and

  (b) the chairing of the council.

(3) A scheme under this Rule may include provision delegating to the district church council such functions of the PCC as are specified in the scheme.

(4) Where there is a scheme under this Rule, the PCC may, subject to the provisions of the scheme, delegate one or more of its functions to the district church council.

(5) But none of the following functions may be delegated under paragraph (3) or (4) –

  (a) functions relating to producing the financial statements of the parish;

  (b) functions under Part 2 of the Patronage (Benefices) Measure 1986 (exercise of rights of presentation);

  (c) functions as an interested party under Part 3 of the Mission and Pastoral Measure 2011 (pastoral schemes etc.).

(6) Where a scheme under this Rule is in operation, the PCC may exercise a function delegated to the district church council under paragraph (3) or (4) despite the delegation.

(7) A scheme under this Rule may provide for –

  (a) the election or choice of one or two deputy churchwardens,

  (b) the delegation by the churchwardens to the deputy or deputies of such functions relating to a church or building licensed for public worship as are specified in the scheme, and

  (c) the deputy or each of the deputies to be an ex officio member of the PCC.

---

* 'Church' means any church or chapel which has been consecrated for the purpose of public worship according to the rites and ceremonies of the Church of England: see section 3, Interpretation Measure 1925.

(8)   A scheme under this Rule may include provision under Rule M34.

(9)   A scheme under this Rule comes into operation on the day specified in the scheme.

(10) Where a scheme is made under this Rule, a copy of the scheme –

(a)   must be filed in the diocesan registry, and

(b)   must be sent to the secretary of the bishop's council and standing committee.

(11) If the parish is in the area of a benefice for which there is a team ministry, each member of the team may attend the meetings of a district church council elected for a district in the parish.

(12) This Rule does not affect the appointment, in parishes with more than one parish church, of two churchwardens for each church under section 1(2)(a) of the Churchwardens Measure 2001.

District church council: disqualification

M36(1)   The provisions of these Rules on disqualification from being nominated, chosen or elected as, or from serving as, a member of the PCC apply also in relation to membership of a district church council established by a scheme under Rule M35 which applies to the parish.

(2)   Any enactment providing for the disqualification of a person from being a trustee of a charity and, accordingly, from being a member of the PCC also has the effect of disqualifying the person from being a member of the district church council.

Section C: Joint Councils

Power to make scheme

M37 (1)   A meeting of the parish and meetings of one or more connected parishes may jointly make a scheme for the establishment of a joint council comprising –

(a)   the minister of each parish to which the scheme applies, and

(b)   representatives of the laity elected, chosen or appointed in the manner and in the numbers specified in the scheme from among the persons each of whom has his or her name on the roll of a parish to which the scheme applies.

(2) The provision which may be made in reliance on Rule 77 (implied power to vary) includes provision for enabling a joint council to include the minister and representatives of one or more other parishes.

(3) A reference in this Section of this Part of these Rules to a meeting of a parish is a reference to the annual meeting or a special parochial church meeting of that parish.

(4) A parish is connected to another parish if –

    (a) they each belong to the same benefice,

    (b) the benefice to which one belongs is held in plurality with the benefice to which the other belongs (whether or not they are held in plurality with one or more other benefices), or

    (c) they are in the area of the same group ministry.

Status, property and functions of joint council

M38(1) A joint council established by a scheme under Rule M37 is a body corporate; and section 3 of the Parochial Church Councils (Powers) Measure 1956 applies to the joint council as if it were a PCC.

(2) A scheme under Rule M37 for the establishment of a joint council must include provision for the transfer from the PCC of each parish to which the scheme applies to the joint council of –

    (a) all property, rights, liabilities and functions, or

    (b) only such property, rights, liabilities and functions as are specified in the scheme.

(3) A scheme under Rule M37 may (in reliance on Rule 77) vary a scheme for the establishment of a joint council by providing for the transfer of specified property, rights, liabilities or functions from the joint council to the PCC of a specified parish to which that scheme applies.

(4) A scheme under Rule M37 may (in reliance on Rule 77) vary a scheme for the establishment of a joint council by providing for that scheme to cease to apply to a specified parish; and the scheme making the variation must include provision for the transfer from the joint council to the PCC for that parish of the property, rights, liabilities and functions concerned.

(5) A scheme under Rule M37 may (in reliance on Rule 77) revoke a scheme for the establishment of a joint council; and the scheme making the revocation must include provision for the transfer from the joint council to the PCC for each parish of the property, rights, liabilities and functions concerned.

(6) A scheme under Rule M37 may make different provision for different purposes and may, in particular, provide for –

(a) transfers of different property, rights, liabilities or functions to take place on different days;

(b) transfers of property, rights, liabilities or functions to take place on different days for different parishes.

(7) Any gift which is expressed as a gift to the PCC of a parish to which a scheme under Rule M37 applies, and which takes effect on or after the relevant transfer date, takes effect as a gift to the joint council, unless all the purposes for which the gift was made relate to functions which continue to be exercisable by the PCC.

(8) In paragraph (7), the 'relevant transfer date' means –

(a) where all the PCC's functions are transferred to the joint council on the same date, that date, or

(b) in any other case, the date or the first date on which one or more of the PCC's functions are transferred to the joint council.

(9) Where a scheme under Rule M37 provides for the transfer of land, the land is, by virtue of the scheme itself and without any further deed or other document, to vest subject to and with the benefit of any tenancies, covenants, conditions, agreements, easements or rights to which the land was subject, and of which it had the benefit, immediately before the transfer took effect.

(10) Where any question arises as to the allocation of property, rights, liabilities or functions to a PCC on a transfer made by virtue of paragraph (3), (4) or (5), the question is to be resolved by the diocesan board of finance for the diocese in which that PCC's parish is situated.

(11) A scheme under Rule M37 does not affect the status of any parish to which the scheme applies or any right which a person has by virtue of being a parishioner or having his or her name on the roll of the parish.

Officers, business etc. of joint council

M39 (1) A scheme under Rule M37 for the establishment of a joint council must include provision for –

(a) the chairing of the joint council,

(b) the meetings of the joint council, and

(c) the procedure of the joint council.

(2) Provision made under paragraph (1)(b) which entitles the representatives of a parish to which the scheme applies to attend a meeting of the joint council and take part in its proceedings does not prevent the holding of a meeting of the parish.

(3) A scheme under Rule M37 may include provision for the membership of a joint council to include persons other than those mentioned in paragraph (1) of that Rule.

(4) A scheme under Rule M37 may include supplementary, transitional or saving provision.

(5) Provision under paragraph (4) may, in particular, apply (with or without modifications) provisions of these Rules or of the Parochial Church Councils (Powers) Measure 1956 or any other provision made by or under a Measure.

Parish ceasing to be connected or being dissolved

M40(1) This Rule applies where a parish to which a scheme under Rule M37 applies ceases, by virtue of a pastoral scheme or order or the termination of provisions of a pastoral scheme or order under section 32(2) of the Mission and Pastoral Measure 2011, to be connected to the other parish or parishes to which the scheme applies.

(2) This Rule also applies where a parish to which a scheme under Rule M37 applies is dissolved by a pastoral scheme which makes provision under section 31(1)(b) of the Mission and Pastoral Measure 2011.

(3) The bishop may by written instrument under his or her hand –

(a) provide for the scheme to cease to apply to the parish which has ceased to be connected to the other parish or parishes or (as the case may be) has been dissolved, or

(b) provide for the scheme to be revoked.

(4) An instrument under this Rule which makes provision under paragraph (3)(a) must also provide for the transfer from the joint council to the PCC for the parish concerned of the property, rights, liabilities and functions concerned.

(5) An instrument under this Rule which makes provision under paragraph (3)(b) must also provide for the transfer from the joint council to the PCC for each of the parishes concerned of the property, rights, liabilities and functions concerned.

(6) Where any question arises as to the allocation of property, rights, liabilities or functions to a PCC on a transfer made by virtue of paragraph (4) or (5), the question is to be resolved by the diocesan board of finance for the diocese in which that PCC's parish is situated.

Disqualification

M41(1) The provisions of these Rules on disqualification from being nominated, chosen or elected as, or from serving as, a member of the PCC apply also in relation to membership of a joint council established by a scheme under Rule M37 to which the parish belongs.

(2) Any enactment providing for the disqualification of a person from being a trustee of a charity and, accordingly, from being a member of the PCC also

has the effect of disqualifying the person from being a member of the joint council.

Procedure for making scheme

M42 (1) A scheme under Rule M37 is valid only if it is approved by at least two-thirds of the persons present and voting at a meeting of each parish to which the scheme applies.

(2) A scheme approved under paragraph (1) by each parish to which it applies must be referred to the bishop's council and standing committee; and the scheme must be accompanied by –

   (a) a copy of the resolution of each meeting at which the scheme was approved, and

   (b) a statement of the number of persons attending each meeting, the number at each meeting voting for approval of the scheme and the number voting against.

(3) The bishop's council and standing committee, having had a scheme referred to it under paragraph (2), may –

   (a) approve the scheme without amendment,

   (b) approve the scheme subject to proposed amendments, or

   (c) decline to approve the scheme.

(4) The bishop's council and standing committee may approve a scheme only if it is satisfied that the scheme makes due provision for the representation on the joint council of the laity of each parish to which the scheme applies.

(5) The provision made in the scheme for the purposes of paragraph (4) must, in particular, include provision for ensuring that the number of clerical members of the joint council does not equal or exceed the number of lay members.

(6) An amendment to a scheme proposed under paragraph (3)(b) is made only if it is approved by at least two-thirds of the persons present and voting at a meeting of each parish to which the scheme applies.

(7) A scheme under Rule M37 comes into operation on the day specified in the scheme.

(8) Where a scheme under Rule M37 is approved under this Rule, a copy of the scheme –

   (a) must be filed in the diocesan registry, and

   (b) must be sent to the secretary of the bishop's council and standing committee.

PART 10: FORMS

Enrolment (see Rules 1(2), (7) and (12) and 7(3) and (5))

Form 1

APPLICATION FOR ENROLMENT ON THE CHURCH ELECTORAL ROLL OF THE PARISH OF:

....

Full Name   ....

Preferred title (if any) ....

Postal Address ....

Postcode ....

Email address (optional) ....

I declare that –

1 I am baptised, am a lay person and am aged 16 or over (or become 16* on

....)

**2A. I am a member of the Church of England or of a Church in communion with the Church of England and am resident in the parish.

OR

2B. I am a member of the Church of England or of a Church in communion with the Church of England, am not resident in the parish, [but have habitually attended public worship in the parish during the preceding six months] [and would have habitually attended public worship in the parish during the preceding six months but was prevented from doing so because. ....]***.

OR

2C. I am a member in good standing of a Church which is not in communion with the Church of England but subscribes to the doctrine of the Holy Trinity, am also a member of the Church of England [and have habitually attended public worship in the parish during the preceding six months] [and would have habitually attended public worship in the parish during the preceding six months but was prevented from doing so because ....]***.

I declare that the above answers are true and I apply for inclusion on the Church Electoral Roll of the parish.

Signed .... Date ....

*A person who is going to become 16 during the next 12 months may complete this Form, and will then be eligible to have his or her name entered on the Roll on his or her 16th birthday.

**Tick only one of 2A, 2B and 2C.

***If you tick 2B or 2C in circumstances where a new Roll is being prepared, you must delete either the first set of words in square brackets or the second set. If you delete the first set, you must complete the second set by filling in the space at the end. See Note 3 for further information.

Notes

General matters

1   The only Churches at present in communion with the Church of England are other Anglican Churches and certain foreign Churches, as listed in the Supplementary Material to the Canons (but note Rule 83(3) of the Church Representation Rules, which provides for any question as to whether a particular Church is in communion with the Church of England to be decided by the Archbishops of Canterbury and York acting jointly).

2   Membership of the electoral roll is also open to members in good standing of a Church not in communion with the Church of England which subscribes to the doctrine of the Holy Trinity where those members are also prepared to declare themselves to be members of the Church of England.

3   Every six years a new roll is prepared and those on the previous roll are informed so that they can reapply. If you are not resident in the parish but were on the roll as a habitual worshipper and have been prevented by illness or other sufficient cause from worshipping for the past six months, you should complete declaration 2B or 2C as follows –
    (a)   delete the first set of words in square brackets and
    (b)   at the end of the second set of words in square brackets, briefly state the reason for not having worshipped as mentioned.

4   If you have any problems with this Form, please approach the clergy or lay people responsible for the parish, who will be pleased to help you.

5   In this Form 'parish' means ecclesiastical parish.

Use of email addresses and other personal data

6 You do not have to provide an email address on this Form. If you do provide one, the Parochial Church Council and the electoral roll officer are entitled to use that email address to communicate with you in connection with the maintenance or revision of the Roll or the preparation of a new Roll or with elections to or membership of the Council.

7 The Church Representation Rules impose certain requirements for your name and address to be given to a third party, such as the diocesan electoral registration officer, in connection with elections to or membership of a deanery synod, diocesan synod or the House of Laity of the General Synod. If you provide an email address on this Form, it will be given to the third party along with your postal address.

8 A third party to whom your name and address have been given under the Church Representation Rules is in certain cases required by the Rules to pass them on to another person, such as the presiding officer in a synodical election. If you provide an email address on this Form, that email address will be given to the other person along with your postal address.

9 Any person to whom your email address or other personal data is given under the Church Representation Rules is required by those Rules to hold the data securely. Furthermore, if you do provide an email address on this Form, that does not give anybody the right to use it for any purpose other than those permitted by the Rules; so it cannot, for example, be used for social matters or fund-raising.

10 The roll is published after each annual revision and after the preparation of a new roll. The published roll will include your name (as well as the name of every other person on the roll) but none of your other personal data (as defined by the Data Protection Act 2018) will be made public as a result of your inclusion on the roll.

Revision of roll (See Rule 3(2))

Form 2

NOTICE OF REVISION OF CHURCH ELECTORAL ROLL

Diocese of ....

Parish of ....

Notice is given that the Church Electoral Roll of the above parish will be revised by the Parochial Church Council, beginning on the .... day of .... 20 .... and ending on the .... day of .... 20 ....*

After the revision, a copy of the Roll will be published by the Parochial Church Council [*method of publication to be specified here*] for at least 14 days and a copy of the Roll will be available for inspection on a reasonable request being made to the Council.

Under the Church Representation Rules, a lay person is entitled to have his or her name entered on the roll if the person –

    (a)   is baptised,

    (b)   is aged 16 or over, and

    (c)   has made one of the following three declarations and duly applied for enrolment.

The first declaration is that the person is a member of the Church of England or of a Church in communion with it and is resident in the parish.

The second declaration is that the person is a member of the Church of England or of a Church in communion with it, is not resident in the parish, but has habitually attended public worship in the parish during the preceding six months.

The third declaration is that the person is a member in good standing of a Church which is not in communion with the Church of England but subscribes to the doctrine of the Holy Trinity and is also a member of the Church of England and has habitually attended public worship in the parish during the preceding six months.

Application Forms for enrolment can be obtained from the Church Electoral Roll Officer. In order for a person to be entitled to attend the annual parochial church meeting and to take part in its proceedings, an Application Form for enrolment must be returned by the date shown above for the ending of the revision of the Church Electoral Roll by the Parochial Church Council.

Any error discovered in the Roll should at once be reported to the Church Electoral Roll Officer.

Dated this ** .... day of .... 20 ....

....
Church Electoral Roll Officer

Address ....

Email address (optional) ....

* The revision must be completed at least 15 days, but no more than 28 days, before the Annual Parochial Church Meeting.
** At least 14 days' notice must be given.

In this Notice, 'parish' means an ecclesiastical parish.

Preparation of new roll (see Rule 6(1))

Form 3

NOTICE OF PREPARATION OF NEW ROLL

Diocese of ....

Parish of ....

Notice is given that under the Church Representation Rules a new Church Electoral Roll* is being prepared. Every person who wishes to have his or her name entered on the new Roll, whether it is entered on the present Roll or not, is requested to apply for enrolment not later than ....

The new Roll will take effect on ....

The new Roll will be published by the Parochial Church Council [*method of publication to be specified here*] for at least 14 days and a copy of the Roll will be available for inspection on a reasonable request being made to the Council.

Under the Church Representation Rules, a lay person is entitled to have his or her name entered on the roll, if the person –
(a)   is baptised,
(b)   is aged 16 or over, and
(c)   has made one of the following three declarations and duly applied for enrolment.

The first declaration is that the person is a member of the Church of England or of a Church in communion with it and is resident in the parish.

The second declaration is that the person is a member of the Church of England or of a Church in communion with it, is not resident in the parish, but has habitually attended public worship in the parish during the preceding six months.

The third declaration is that the person is a member in good standing of a Church which is not in communion with the Church of England but subscribes to the doctrine of the Holy Trinity and is also a member of the Church of England and has habitually attended public worship in the parish during the preceding six months.

Application Forms for enrolment can be obtained from the Church Electoral Roll Officer. In order to be entitled to attend the annual parochial church meeting and to take part in its proceedings, you must return the Application Form for enrolment by the earlier of the dates given above.

Any error discovered in the roll should at once be reported to the Church Electoral Roll Officer.

Dated this .... day of .... 20 ......

....
Church Electoral Roll Officer

Address ....

Email address (optional) ....

* The new roll must be completed at least 15 days, but no more than 28 days, before the Annual Parochial Church Meeting.

In this Notice, 'parish' means an ecclesiastical parish.

Election to diocesan synod (see Rule 40(3))

Form 4

NOTICE OF ELECTION TO HOUSE OF CLERGY OR HOUSE OF LAITY OF DIOCESAN SYNOD

Diocese of ....

Deanery of ....

1   An election of .... members of the House of Clergy/Laity of the Diocesan Synod will be held in the above Deanery on ....

2   Every candidate must be nominated by two qualified electors on forms to be obtained from ....
All members, other than co-opted members, of the House of Clergy/Laity of the deanery synod are qualified electors. Each qualified elector nominating must be a member of the House of Clergy/Laity of the deanery synod to which the candidate belongs.

3   For the qualifications to be a candidate for election to the House of Clergy/Laity of the diocesan synod, see Rule 36 of the Church Representation Rules.

4   The election will be decided by simple majority/the single transferable vote.

Nomination for election to diocesan synod (see Rule 40(3))

Form 5

NOMINATION TO HOUSE OF CLERGY OR HOUSE OF LAITY OF DIOCESAN SYNOD

Diocese of ....

Deanery of ....

Election of members of the House of Clergy/Laity of the Diocesan Synod

We the proposer and seconder, each being qualified electors and members of the House of Clergy/Laity of the Deanery Synod for the above Deanery, nominate the following person as a candidate at the election in the above Deanery.

Surname	Christian Names	Postal address	Email address	Year of Birth

Proposer's signature ....

Proposer's full name ....

Address ....

Seconder's signature ....

Seconder's full name ....

Address ....

I, the above named .... declare that I am not subject to any disqualification referred to in the Notes on this form and signify my willingness to serve as a member of the House of Clergy/Laity of the Diocesan Synod if elected.

Candidate's signature ....

This nomination must be sent to ....

Notes

1   All members, other than co-opted members, of the House of Clergy/Laity of the deanery synod are qualified electors.

2   (1) A person is disqualified from being nominated for membership of a diocesan synod if the person is included in a barred list (within the meaning of the Safeguarding Vulnerable Groups Act 2006).

     (2) A person is disqualified from being nominated for membership of any Synod if the person has been convicted of an offence mentioned in Schedule 1 to the Children and Young Persons Act 1933 (with that expression being construed in accordance with Rule 71(2) of the Church Representation Rules).

     (3) A person's disqualification under sub-paragraph (2) may be waived by the bishop of the diocese by giving the person notice in writing.

Voting paper for election to diocesan synod (see Rule 42(1) and (8)

Form 6

VOTING PAPER FOR ELECTION TO HOUSE OF CLERGY OR HOUSE OF LAITY OF DIOCESAN SYNOD (SIMPLE MAJORITY SYSTEM)

.... Diocesan Synod

Election of members of the House of Clergy/Laity

Deanery of ....

.... members to be elected.

Voting Paper

Mark your vote in this column	Candidates' names, addresses and year of birth

Guidance to Voters

1   The voting paper must be signed and the full name written on the reverse.
2   You have as many votes as there are members to be elected.
3   You may not give more than one vote to any one candidate.
4   You vote by placing an 'X' opposite the name(s) of the candidate(s) of your choice.
5   If you inadvertently spoil your voting paper you may return it to the Presiding Officer who will give you another paper.
6   This voting paper duly completed on the reverse must be delivered (by post or otherwise) to .... so as to arrive by no later than ....

The following to be printed on back of form –

Signature of voter ....

Full name ....

Address ....

....

Alternative voting paper for election to diocesan synod (See Rule 42(1) and (9)

Form 7

VOTING PAPER FOR ELECTION TO HOUSE OF CLERGY OR HOUSE OF LAITY OF DIOCESAN SYNOD (STV SYSTEM)

.... Diocesan Synod

Election of members of the House of Clergy/Laity

Deanery of ....

.... members to be elected.

Voting Paper

Mark your vote in this column	Candidates' names, addresses and year of birth

Guidance to Voters

1   The voting paper must be signed and the full name written on the reverse.

2   Use your single transferable vote by entering '1' against your first preference, and if desired, '2' against your second preference, '3' against your third preference, and so on as far as you wish. The sequence of your preferences is crucial. NO CROSS should be used.

3   You should continue to express preferences for as long as you are able to place successive candidates in order. A later preference is considered only if an earlier preference either has a surplus above the quota (the minimum number required to guarantee election) or has been excluded because of insufficient support.

4   The numbering of your preferences must be consecutive and given to different candidates. Remember that marking a second or subsequent preference cannot affect the chances of any earlier preference.

5   If you inadvertently spoil your voting paper you may return it to the Presiding Officer who will give you another paper.

6   This voting paper duly completed on the reverse thereof must be delivered (by post or otherwise) to .... so as to arrive by no later than ....

The following to be printed on back of form –

Signature of voter ....

Full name ....

Address ....

Annual meeting (see Rule M2(1))

Form M1

NOTICE OF ANNUAL PAROCHIAL CHURCH MEETING

Parish of ....

The Annual Parochial Church Meeting will be held in ....

....

on the .... day of .... 20......... at ....

For election of parochial representatives of the laity as follows –

*To the Deanery Synod .... representatives.

To the Parochial Church Council .... representatives.

For the appointment of the Independent Examiner or Auditor.

For the consideration of:
(a)   a report on changes to the Roll since the last annual parochial church meeting OR** a report on the numbers entered on the new Roll;
(b)   an Annual Report on the proceedings of the parochial church council and the activities of the parish generally;
(c)   the financial statements of the council for the year ending on the 31st December preceding the meeting;
(d)   the annual report on the fabric, goods and ornaments of the church or churches of the parish;
(e)   a report of the proceedings of the deanery synod; and
(f)   other matters of parochial or general Church interest.

In this Notice, 'parish' means an ecclesiastical parish.

* To be included in a year in which parochial representatives of the laity are to be elected to the Deanery Synod.
** To be included in a year when a new Church Electoral Roll is prepared. Delete as applicable.

Notes
1   Every lay person whose name is entered on the Church Electoral Roll of the parish (and no other person) is entitled to vote at the election of parochial representatives of the laity.

2   A person is qualified to be elected a parochial representative of the laity if –
        (a) his or her name is entered on the Church Electoral Roll of the parish and, unless he or is under 18, has been entered there for at least the preceding six months;

(b) he or she is an actual communicant (which means that he has received Communion according to the use of the Church of England or of a Church in communion with the Church of England at least three times during the twelve months preceding the date of the election);

(c) he or she is at least 16; and

(d) he or she is not disqualified as referred to in paragraph 3 of these Notes.

3   (1) A person is disqualified from being nominated, chosen or elected or from serving as a churchwarden or a member of a parochial church council, a district church council or a joint council if the person is disqualified from being a trustee of a charity (and the disqualification is not subject to a waiver which permits membership of a parochial church council, district church council or joint council).

(2) A person is disqualified from being nominated, chosen or elected or from serving as a member of a parochial church council, a district church council, a joint council or a deanery synod if the person is included in a barred list (within the meaning of the Safeguarding Vulnerable Groups Act 2006).

(3) A person is disqualified from being nominated, chosen or elected or from serving as a member of a parochial church council, a district church council, a joint council or a deanery synod if the person has been convicted of an offence mentioned in Schedule 1 to the Children and Young Persons Act 1933 (with that expression being construed in accordance with Rule 71(2) of the Church Representation Rules).

(4) A person's disqualification under sub-paragraph (3) may be waived by the bishop of the diocese by giving the person notice in writing.

(5) A person is disqualified from being nominated, chosen or elected or from serving as a member of a parochial church council if the person has been disqualified from holding office under section 10(6) of the Incumbent (Vacation of Benefices) Measure 1977.

4*   A scheme is in operation in this parish which provides that any person entitled to vote in the elections of parochial representatives of the laity to the parochial church council or to the deanery synod or to both may apply on the appropriate form to the Minister of the parish (or other person signing below) for a postal vote. The completed form must be received before the commencement of the annual parochial church meeting.

Signed ....

Minister of the parish**

* This paragraph should be deleted if no scheme for postal voting is in operation in the parish.

** Or vice-chair of the parochial church council as the case may be (see Rule M19(2) of the Church Representation Rules).

Postal vote (see Rule M11(1) and (5))

Form M2

APPLICATION FOR POSTAL VOTE

Parish of ....

I .... (full Christian name and surname)

of.. (address)

declare that my name is entered on the church electoral roll of the above parish and I apply for a postal vote in any elections to which postal voting applies to be held at the forthcoming annual parochial church meeting for the parish.

The voting paper should be given to me at the above address OR* at the following address –
....

Dated .... 20 ....

Signed ....

* Delete as appropriate.

PART 11

INDEX

Each of the following expressions is defined or otherwise glossed or explained in the provision specified in the following Table –

Supplementary Material

(not forming part of the Rules)

Churchwardens Measure 2001

Number and qualifications of churchwardens

1 (1)   Subject to the provisions of this Measure there shall be two churchwardens of every parish.

(2)(a)   Where by virtue of a designation made by a pastoral scheme or otherwise a parish has more than one parish church, two churchwardens shall be appointed for each of the parish churches, and this Measure shall apply separately to each pair of churchwardens, but all the churchwardens shall be churchwardens of the whole parish except so far as they may arrange to perform separate duties in relation to the several parish churches.

(b)   A church building or part of a building designated as a parish centre of worship under section 29(2) of the Pastoral Measure 1983 (1983 No. 1) shall, subject to subsection (4) of that section, be deemed while the designation is in force to be a parish church for the purposes of this subsection.

(3)   The churchwardens of every parish shall be chosen from persons who have been baptised and –

(a)   whose names are on the church electoral roll of the parish;

(b)   who are actual communicants;

(c)   who are twenty-one years of age or upwards; and

(d)   who are not disqualified under section 2 or 3 below.

(4)   If it appears to the bishop, in the case of any particular person who is not qualified by virtue of paragraph (a), (b) or (c) of subsection (3) above, that there are exceptional circumstances which justify a departure from the requirements of those paragraphs the bishop may permit that person to hold the office of churchwarden notwithstanding that those requirements are not met. Any such permission shall apply only to the period of office next following the date on which the permission is given.

(5)   No person shall be chosen as churchwarden of a parish for any period of office unless he –

(a) has signified consent to serve as such; and

(b) has not signified consent to serve as such for the same period of office in any other parish (not being a related parish) or, if such consent has been signified and the meeting of the parishioners to elect churchwardens of that other parish has been held, was not chosen as churchwarden of that other parish.

In this subsection 'related parish' means a parish –

(a) belonging to the benefice to which the first-mentioned parish belongs; or

(b) belonging to a benefice held in plurality with the benefice to which the first-mentioned parish belongs; or

(c) having the same minister as the first-mentioned parish.

(6)   In relation to the filling of a casual vacancy among the churchwardens the reference in subsection (5)(b) above to the same period of office shall be construed as a reference to a period of office which includes the period for which the casual vacancy is to be filled.

General disqualifications

2 (1) A person shall be disqualified from being chosen for the office of churchwarden if –

(a) he is disqualified from being a charity trustee under section 72(1) of the Charities Act 1993 (c. 10) and the disqualification is not for the time being subject to a general waiver by the Charity Commission under section 178 of the Charities Act 2011 and the disqualification is not for the time being subject to a general waiver by the Charity Commission under section 181 of that Act or to a waiver by it under that section in respect of all ecclesiastical charities established for purposes relating to the parish concerned or

(b) the person is disqualified from being a charity trustee by an order under section 181A of that Act.

In this subsection 'ecclesiastical charity' has the same meaning as that assigned to that expression in the Local Government Act 1894 (c. 73).

(1A) A person shall be disqualified from being chosen for the office of churchwarden if the person is included in a barred list (within the meaning of the Safeguarding Vulnerable Groups Act 2006).

(2)(a) A person shall be disqualified from being chosen for the office of churchwarden if he has been convicted of any offence mentioned in Schedule 1 to the Children and Young Persons Act 1933 (c. 12).

(b) [Repealed by Safeguarding and Clergy Discipline Measure 2016 (No. 1).]

(3) A person shall be disqualified from being chosen for the office of churchwarden if he is disqualified from holding that office under section 10(6) of the Incumbents (Vacation of Benefices) Measure 1977 (No. 1).

(3A) A person's disqualification under subsection (2)(a) may be waived by the bishop serving written notice on the person; and the notice must specify the bishop's reasons for giving the waiver.

(3B) A waiver under subsection (3A) –

(a) is of unlimited duration, and

(b) has effect in every diocese.

(3C) Before deciding whether to give a waiver under subsection (3A), the bishop must consult –

(a) the diocesan safeguarding advisor, and

(b) such other persons as the bishop considers appropriate.

(3D) On serving a notice under subsection (3A), the bishop shall give a copy of the notice to the registrar of the diocese; and the registrar shall file the copy in the diocesan registry.

(4) All rules of law whereby certain persons are disqualified from being chosen for the office of churchwarden shall cease to have effect.

Disqualification after six periods of office

3 Without prejudice to section 2 above, a person shall be disqualified from being chosen for the office of churchwarden when that person has served as a churchwarden of the same parish for six successive periods of office until the annual meeting of the parishioners to elect churchwardens in the next year but one following the date on which that person vacated office at the end of the last such period:

Provided that a meeting of the parishioners may by resolution decide that this section shall not apply in relation to the parish concerned.

Any such resolution may be revoked by a subsequent meeting of the parishioners.

Time and manner of choosing

4 (1) The churchwardens of a parish shall be chosen annually not later than 31st May in each year.

(2) Subject to the provisions of this Measure the churchwardens of a parish shall be elected by a meeting of the parishioners.

(3) Candidates for election at the meeting must be nominated and seconded in writing by persons entitled to attend the meeting and each nomination paper must include a statement, signed by the person nominated, to the effect that that person is willing to serve as a churchwarden and is

not disqualified under section 2(1), (1A), (2) or (3) above.

(4) A nomination shall not be valid unless –

(a) the nomination paper is received by the minister of the parish before the commencement of the meeting; and

(b) in the case of a person who is not qualified by virtue of section 1(3)(a), (b) or (c) above, the bishop's permission was given under section 1(4) above before the nomination paper is received by the minister of the parish.

(5) If it appears to the minister of the parish that the election of any particular person nominated might give rise to serious difficulties between the minister and that person in the carrying out of their respective functions the minister may, before the election is conducted, make a statement to the effect that only one churchwarden is to be elected by the meeting. In that event one churchwarden shall be appointed by the minister from among the persons nominated, the name of the person so appointed being announced before the election is conducted, and the other shall then be elected by the meeting.

(6) During any period when there is no minister –

(a) subsection (4) above shall apply with the substitution for the words 'minister of the parish' of the words 'churchwarden by whom the notice convening the meeting was signed'; and

(b) subsection (5) above shall not apply.

(7) A person may be chosen to fill a casual vacancy among the churchwardens at any time.

(8) Any person chosen to fill a casual vacancy shall be chosen in the same manner as was the churchwarden whose place he is to fill except that, where the churchwarden concerned was appointed by the minister and the minister has ceased to hold office, the new churchwarden to fill the casual vacancy shall be elected by a meeting of the parishioners.

Meeting of the parishioners

5 (1) A joint meeting of –

(a) the persons whose names are entered on the church electoral roll of the parish; and

(b) the persons resident in the parish whose names are entered on a register of local government electors by reason of such residence,

shall be deemed to be a meeting of the parishioners for the purposes of this Measure.

(2) The meeting of the parishioners shall be convened by the minister or, during any period when there is no minister or when the minister is unable or unwilling to do so, the churchwardens of the parish by a notice signed by the minister or a churchwarden as the case may be.

(3) The notice shall state the place, day and hour at which the meeting of the parishioners is to be held; and the notice must also include an explanation of the right of appeal under section 5A against the result of the election.

(4) The notice shall, for a period including the last two Sundays before the meeting, be displayed –

(a) in the case of the parish church or, where there is more than one church in the parish, each of those churches, on or near the principal door, and

(b) in the case of each building in the parish licensed for public worship, in a location readily visible to members of the congregation.

(5) The minister, if present, or, if he is not present, a chairman chosen by the meeting of the parishioners, shall preside thereat.

(6) In case of an equal division of votes on any question other than one to determine an election of a churchwarden the chairman of the meeting of parishioners shall not have a second or casting vote and the motion on that question shall be treated as lost.

(7) The Church Representation Rules contained in Schedule 3 to the Synodical Government Measure 1969 (No. 1) may provide for the procedure to be followed at a meeting of the parishioners for the purposes of this Measure and, subject to any provision in the Rules, the meeting has

power to adjourn and to determine its own rules of procedure.

(8) A person appointed by the meeting of the parishioners shall act as clerk of the meeting and shall record the minutes thereof.

Election appeal

5A (1) An appeal may be made against the result of an election under section 4 on the grounds that a person whose election is the subject of the appeal –

    (a) was not duly elected,

    (b) was not qualified to be a candidate at the time of the election, or

    (c) before the election was held, misrepresented a material fact in connection with the election.

(2) An appeal may be made against the result of an election under section 4 on the grounds that the conduct of the election was such as to affect the outcome of the election.

(3) An appeal may be made against the result of an election under section 4 on the grounds that –

    (a) it has been determined on an appeal under Rule 57 of the Church Representation Rules that an error was made in the roll or the question is awaiting determination on an appeal under that Rule, and

    (b) the error would or might be material to the result of the election.

(4) An appeal may be made against the result of an election under section 4 on the grounds that a vote which was allowed should have been disallowed, or that a vote which was disallowed should have been allowed, but only if the allowance or disallowance of the vote would or might be material to the result of the election.

(5) An appeal under this section may be made by –

    (a) a person entitled to take part in the meeting of the parishioners for making the election, or

    (b) a candidate in the election.

(6) Notice of an appeal under this section –

    (a) must be in writing,

    (b) must give brief particulars of the grounds of the appeal, and

    (c) may be accompanied by written submissions.

(7) Notice of an appeal under this section must be given to the lay chair of the deanery synod (as defined by Rule 26(7) of the Church Representation Rules).

(8) On an appeal under this section, a person who was declared elected but whose election is or may be affected by the appeal is to be regarded for all purposes as elected pending the determination of the appeal.

(9) Rules 60 to 60C and 61I of the Church Representation Rules apply to an appeal under subsection (1)(a) or (b) or (4) of this section as they apply respectively to an appeal under Rule 58A(1)(a) or (b) or (4) of those Rules (summary election appeal).

(10) Rules 61 to 61I of the Church Representation Rules apply to an appeal under subsection (1)(c), (2) or (3) of this section as they apply respectively to an appeal under Rule 58A(1)(c), (2) or (3) of those Rules (full election appeal).

Admission

6(1) At a time and place to be appointed by the bishop annually, being on a date not later than 31st August in each year, each person chosen for the office of churchwarden shall appear before the bishop or his substitute duly appointed, and be admitted to the office of churchwarden after –

    (a) making a declaration, in the presence of the bishop or his substitute, that he will faithfully and diligently perform the duties of his office; and

    (b) subscribing a declaration to that effect and also that he is not disqualified under section 2(1), (1A), (2) or (3) above.

No person chosen for the office of churchwarden shall become churchwarden until such time as he shall have been admitted to office in accordance with the provisions of this section.

(2) Subject to the provisions of this Measure the term of office of the churchwardens so chosen and admitted as aforesaid shall

continue until a date determined as follows, that is to say –

(a) in the case of a person who is chosen again as churchwarden at the next annual meeting of the parishioners –

   (i) if so admitted for the next term of office by 31st August in the year in question, the date of the admission; or

   (ii) if not so admitted for the next term of office by 31st August in the year in question, that date;

(b) in the case of a person who is not chosen again as churchwarden at the next annual meeting of the parishioners –

   (i) if that person's successor in office is so admitted for the next term of office by 31st August in the year in question, the date of the admission; or

   (ii) if that person's successor in office is not so admitted for the next term of office by 31st August in the year in question, that date.

In the application of paragraph (b) above to any person, where there is doubt as to which of the new churchwardens is that person's successor in office the bishop may designate one of the new churchwardens as that person's successor for the purposes of that paragraph.

(3) Where any person ceases to hold the office of churchwarden at the end of August in any year by virtue of paragraph (a)(ii) or (b)(ii) above a casual vacancy in that office shall be deemed to have arisen.

(4) In relation to the filling of a casual vacancy the reference in subsection (1) above to 31st August shall be construed as a reference to a date three months after the person who is to fill the vacancy is chosen or the date of the next annual meeting of the parishioners to elect churchwardens, whichever is the earlier.

Suspension

6A (1) This section applies where –

(a) a churchwarden is arrested on suspicion of committing an offence mentioned in Schedule 1 to the Children and Young Persons Act 1933 or is charged with such an offence without being arrested, or

(b) the bishop is satisfied, on the basis of information provided by a local authority or the police, that a churchwarden presents a significant risk of harm.

(2) The bishop may suspend the person from the office of churchwarden by serving written notice on the person; and the notice must specify the bishop's reasons for imposing the suspension.

(3) The bishop may at any time revoke a suspension under this section by serving written notice on the person.

(4) For the purposes of subsection (1)(b), a person presents a significant risk of harm if there is a significant risk that the person may –

(a) harm a child or vulnerable adult,

(b) cause a child or vulnerable adult to be harmed,

(c) put a child or vulnerable adult at risk of harm,

(d) attempt to harm a child or vulnerable adult, or

(e) incite another person to harm a child or vulnerable adult.

(5) Before deciding whether to suspend a person in reliance on subsection (1)(b) or whether to revoke a suspension made in reliance on subsection (1)(b), the bishop must consult –

(a) the diocesan safeguarding advisor, and

(b) such other persons as the bishop considers appropriate.

(6) Where, in reliance on subsection (1)(a), a notice of suspension is served under subsection (2) and the suspension has not been revoked under subsection (3), the suspension continues until the earlier of –

(a) the expiry of three months beginning with the day on which the notice is served, and

(b) the conclusion of the matter.

(7) If, in the case of a suspension made in reliance on subsection (1)(a), the matter is not concluded before the expiry of the period referred to in subsection (6)(a), a further notice of suspension under subsection (2) may be served on the person; and subsection (6) and this subsection apply

to the further suspension as they applied to the earlier suspension or suspensions.

(8) Where, in reliance on subsection (1)(b), a notice of suspension is served under subsection (2) and the suspension has not been revoked under subsection (3), the suspension continues until the expiry of three months beginning with the day on which the notice is served.

(9) In the case of a suspension made in reliance on subsection (1)(b), a further notice of suspension under subsection (2) may be served on the person; and subsection (8) and this subsection apply to the further suspension as they applied to the earlier suspension or suspensions.

(10) Having served a notice of suspension or revocation under this section, the bishop shall give each of the following written notification –

(a) the archdeacon of each archdeaconry in the diocese,

(b) the rural dean or the area dean of the deanery in which the parish in question is situated,

(c) the clergy who hold office in the parish,

(d) the other churchwarden or churchwardens of the parish,

(e) each suffragan bishop of the diocese,

(f) the registrar of the diocese,

(g) the diocesan safeguarding advisor, and

(h) such other persons as the bishop considers appropriate.

(11) The registrar shall file the notification given under subsection (10)(f) in the diocesan registry.

(12) For the purposes of this section, a matter is concluded when –

(a) a decision is taken not to charge the person with the offence in question, or

(b) where the person is charged with the offence, the proceedings for the offence are concluded.

(13) In this section –

'child' means a person aged under 18;

'vulnerable adult' has the same meaning

as in the Safeguarding and Clergy Discipline Measure 2016.

Appeal against suspension under section 6A

6B (1) A person on whom a notice of suspension is served under section 6A(2) may appeal against the suspension to the president of tribunals.

(2) On an appeal under this section, the president of tribunals may, within 28 days following the lodging of the appeal, either confirm or revoke the suspension.

Resignation

7(1) A person may resign the office of churchwarden in accordance with the following provisions of this section, but not otherwise.

(2) Written notice of intention to resign shall be served on the bishop by post.

(3) The resignation shall have effect and the office shall be vacated –

(a) at the end of the period of two months following service of the notice on the bishop; or

(b) on such earlier date as may be determined by the bishop after consultation with the minister and any other churchwarden of the parish.

Vacation of office

8(1) The office of churchwarden of a parish shall be vacated if –

(a) the name of the person concerned is removed from the church electoral roll of the parish under Rule 4 of the Church Representation Rules; or

(b) the name of the person concerned is not on a new church electoral roll of the parish prepared under Rule 7 of those Rules; or

(c) the churchwarden becomes disqualified under section 2(1), (1A), (2) or (3) above.

(1A) Where the office of churchwarden is vacated under subsection (1)(c) on a person being disqualified under section 2(2)(a), the person may resume the office if the disqualification is waived under section 2(3A) and if the office has remained vacant.

(2) For the purposes of this section a person who has been chosen for the office of churchwarden but has not yet been admitted to that office shall be deemed to hold that office, and the expressions 'office' and 'churchwarden' shall be construed accordingly.

Guild churches

9 (1) In the case of every church in the City of London designated and established as a Guild Church under the City of London (Guild Churches) Acts 1952 and 1960 the churchwardens shall, notwithstanding anything to the contrary contained in those Acts, be actual communicant members of the Church of England except where the bishop shall otherwise permit.

(2) Subject to subsection (1) above, nothing in this Measure shall apply to the churchwardens of any church designated and established as a Guild church under the City of London (Guild Churches) Acts 1952 and 1960.

(3) In this section 'actual communicant member of the Church of England' means a member of the Church of England who is confirmed or ready and desirous of being confirmed and has received Communion according to the use of the Church of England or of a church in communion with the Church of England at least three times during the twelve months preceding the date of his election or appointment.

Special provisions

10 (1) In the carrying out of the provisions of this Measure the bishop shall have power –

(a) to make provision for any matter not herein provided for;

(b) to appoint a person to do any act in respect of which there has been any neglect or default on the part of any person or body charged with any duty under this Measure;

(c) so far as may be necessary for the purpose of giving effect to the intentions of this Measure, to extend or alter the time for holding any meeting or election or to modify the procedure laid down by this Measure in connection therewith;

(d) in any case in which there has been no valid choice to direct a fresh choice to

be made, and to give such directions in connection therewith as he may think necessary; and

(e) in any case in which any difficulty arises, to give any directions which he may consider expedient for the purpose of removing the difficulty.

(2) The powers of the bishop under this section shall not enable him to validate anything that was invalid at the time it was done.

Savings

11(1) Subject to section 9 above, nothing in this Measure shall be deemed to amend, repeal or affect any local act or any scheme made under any enactment affecting the churchwardens of a parish:

Provided that for the purposes of this Measure the Parish of Manchester Division Act 1850 (13 & 14 Vict. c. 41) shall be deemed to be a general act.

(2) Subject to section 12 below, in the case of any parish where there is an existing custom which regulates the number of churchwardens or the manner in which the churchwardens are chosen, nothing in this Measure shall affect that custom:

Provided that in the case of any parish where in accordance with that custom any churchwarden was, before the coming into force of the Churchwardens (Appointment and Resignation) Measure 1964 (No. 3), chosen by the vestry of that parish jointly with any other person or persons that churchwarden shall be chosen by the meeting of the parishioners jointly with the other person or persons.

Abolition of existing customs

12 (1) A meeting of the parishioners of a parish may pass a resolution abolishing any existing custom which regulates the number of churchwardens of the parish or the manner in which the churchwardens of the parish are chosen.

(2) Where any such resolution is passed the existing custom to which it relates shall cease to have effect on the date on which the next meeting of parishioners by which the churchwardens are to be elected is held.

(3) In the case of an existing custom which involves a person other than the minister in the choice of the churchwardens, a resolution under subsection (1) above shall not be passed without the written consent of that person.

Interpretation

13 (1) In this Measure, except in so far as the context otherwise requires –

'bishop' means the diocesan bishop concerned;

'diocesan safeguarding advisor' means the person appointed as such for the diocese in question in accordance with provision made by Canon;

'existing custom' means a custom existing at the coming into force of this Measure which has continued for a period commencing before 1st January 1925;

'minister' has the same meaning as that assigned to that expression in Rule 83(1) of the Church Representation Rules except that, where a special responsibility for pastoral care in respect of the parish in question has been assigned to a member of the team in a team ministry under section 20(8A) of the Pastoral Measure 1983 (1983 No. 1) but a special cure of souls in respect of the parish has not been assigned to a vicar in the team ministry by a scheme under that Measure or by his licence from the bishop, it means that member;

'pastoral scheme' has the same meaning as that assigned to that expression in section 87(1) of the Pastoral Measure 1983;

'actual communicant', 'parish' and 'public worship' each have the same meaning as in the Church Representation Rules (see Rules 82 and 83).

(1A) A reference in this Measure to an offence mentioned in Schedule 1 to the Children and Young Persons Act 1933 is a reference to an offence which is –

(a) mentioned in that Schedule as amended, extended or applied from time to time, or

(b) treated by an enactment (whenever passed or made) as if it were mentioned in that Schedule.

(2) Where by virtue of any custom existing at the coming into force of the Churchwardens (Appointment and Resignation) Measure 1964 (1964 No. 3) the choice of a churchwarden was, under section 12(2) of that Measure, required to be made by the meeting of the parishioners jointly with another person or persons that custom shall be deemed to be an existing custom for the purposes of this Measure.

Transitional provisions

[REPEALED BY STATUTE LAW (REPEALS) MEASURE 2018 (NO.1).]

Consequential amendment and repeals

15 (1) The enactment mentioned in Schedule 2 to this Measure shall have effect subject to the consequential amendment specified in that Schedule.

(2) The enactments mentioned in Schedule 3 to this Measure are hereby repealed to the extent specified in the third column of that Schedule.

Short title, commencement and extent

16 (1) This Measure may be cited as the Churchwardens Measure 2001.

(2) This Measure shall come into force on such day as the Archbishops of Canterbury and York may jointly appoint, and different days may be appointed for different provisions.

(3) This Measure shall extend to the whole of the Provinces of Canterbury and York except the Channel Islands and the Isle of Man, but the provisions thereof may be applied to the Channel Islands as defined in the Channel Islands (Church Legislation) Measures 1931 and 1957, or either of them, in accordance with those Measures and if an Act of Tynwald or an instrument made in pursuance of an Act of Tynwald so provides, shall extend to the Isle of Man subject to such exceptions, adaptations or modifications as may be specified in the Act of Tynwald or instrument.

Schedule 1 has been repealed.

Schedule 2 and 3 deal with consequential amendments and repeals and are not reproduced here.

Index